DAD'S WAR

BY ANDY CROPPER

Dedicated to some very precious memories
and to all those ordinary soldiers who
"had a fairly uneventful war, really".

ANDY CROPPER

JOHN CROPPER

NUMBER 209/500

ANMAS PUBLICATIONS
SEPTEMBER 1994

PUBLISHED BY
ANMAS PUBLICATIONS
'WOODLANDS' THE PROSPECT,
ROCKSIDE ROAD, THURLSTONE
S30 6RA

Printed and bound by:
B&B Press (Parkgate) Limited
Aldwarke Road, Parkgate, Rotherham S62 6DY

ISBN 0 9524222 0 4

CONTENTS

PAGE

Introduction 4

Chapter 1 -   From Blue to Khaki   8

Chapter 2 -   Practice Makes Perfect   16

Chapter 3 -   And So To War   22

Chapter 4 -   Promotion   27

Chapter 5 -   A Test Of Nerve   36

Chapter 6 -   Count Your Dead   46

Chapter 7 -   Casualties Of War   57

Chapter 8 -   A Reluctant Command   69

Chapter 9 -   The Final Push   79

Chapter 10 - Farewell Old Friend   90

Chapter 11 - And Back To Blue   101

Addendum - 106

Bibliography - 107

Acknowledgements - 108

INTRODUCTION

In common with many history students I am used to reading detailed records of military formations, daring deeds of decorated servicemen and life histories of some of the most senior members of the armed forces, both past and present. I can quote regulation uniforms for selected units and have a good knowledge of the arms and equipment they carried. I can also tell you about the course of famous, and not so famous, battles.

Like most people with an interest in matters military I acquired this knowledge through extensive reading, visits to museums, films and tales told me by my peers and elders. At the beginning it was always the 'big picture' I wanted. The Charge of the Light Brigade, El Alamein and Waterloo. Such general information was, and still is, generally available. But as my interest and knowledge increased, a desire for more detailed information grew. Just as to a classical music buff who looks on Beethoven's Moonlight Sonata as Sonata No. 14, Opus 27 No. 2 in C sharp minor, I came to refer to the Accrington Pals as the 11th (Service) Battalion (Accrington) East Lancashire Regiment. This thirst for detailed information grips you, it certainly gripped me.

The next stage then became the most rewarding of all. In recent years many of the diaries written by participants in the Great War have become available. Knowledge of the big picture is one thing, but it only comes into context when you become privy to the thoughts, the fears and the hopes of a common soldier caught up in these monumental events. Diaries from earlier wars are also more easily acquired now as are those from later this century and collectively they form a very pertinent, lasting and important record of man's (and woman's) resilience and adaptability.

They also teach us much of the futility of war, highlighting the fact that the common people, who form 99% of the world's population, can become embroiled in actions they would take no part in given a free choice. When you read the front line soldiers' diaries of the two world wars we had this century, if it were not for the difference in language they could easily have been written by people sitting in the same hole and fighting on the same side. They were just simple individuals carried along with events and finding themselves at the very point of conflict. Only their nationality dictated the colours they wore and the weapons they carried. Not for them the stress of diplomacy, of diplomatic threats and counter-threats. Of anger whilst sitting down to a full breakfast table on learning the extent of the previous day's losses. They did it for real.

It's sad to think that mankind can keep going down the same old route time and time again. And it would be foolish to think that the onset of war or 'policing actions' as they are now termed will ever truly end. It would be equally foolish not to take heed of what happened in the past though, for it is only with greater knowledge that we can ever control this seemingly inbuilt desire for martial supremacy and the destruction of our fellow man.

For this reason I make no excuses for my own interest. Yes, I too am fascinated by the 'glory', but over the years I have come to learn that the reality for the participants in those 'glorious' actions, such as Rorke's Drift or Balaklava, was more a feeling of relief at having survived and the hope that now they have done their bit they can go home. Not to detract in any way from their achievements against often unimaginable odds, or from those for whom fear held no place in their lives, but given the choice few would wish to sit in a hole with shells falling around or march in a line towards an unseen foe with the air full of flying metal. Yet ordinary people have done and will doubtless continue to do so.

The fullest understanding can only come from examining as much information as you can so for me, therefore, it mattered not whether the writer had partaken in any particular action, had reached an exalted rank or was the beneficiary of some high award. Indeed it was often more interesting if he had not, for the vast majority of participants did not fit these categories. The very fact that he or she had recorded what happened to them as an individual, within military surroundings, made this information of extreme importance.

To learn that one particular soldier had softened his new boots by going for a march in them, without socks, and then sitting with his feet in a cool stream for 30 minutes before taking them off is wonderful. To learn that another blancoed his brass buttons in the belief it would make them look like bakelite is priceless. This brings everything to life and builds an understanding beyond army regulations and tactical theory.

I thus began a search for personal memoirs, of any era. It didn't matter if the writer spent his service on an anti-aircraft battery in Scapa Flow or had found himself participating in one of the more famous 'battles', just so long as it included details of the day to day lifestyle, the ups and downs, the good times and bad. The real face of war. This, to me, became a chronicle of what it was all about.

My major period of interest has always been the Great War and I have often lamented the fact that whilst there were many survivors still alive this had never been a 'popular' period in our history and many experiences, tales and memories have now been lost to us forever simply because no-one asked the question and recorded the answer. Now, more than 75 years after that war ended, researchers raise more questions than answers because there are precious few left who can speak from actual experience and many written documents have simply been thrown away in the belief that they were unwanted.

Indeed, I recently discovered that 5 years worth of letters from the Great War, written by a Kitchener recruit who fought in almost every major action on the western front and who ended up with a field commission, were committed to a rubbish tip just a few years ago. A common occurrence no doubt, but particularly painful for me as they were written by my Uncle Tom.

Tom is sadly not around any more to fill in the blanks of his experiences but that discovery made me realise that the same will soon happen with the veterans of World War II although thankfully, from a researcher's point of view, others have realised this too and many books and articles are starting to appear.

In all my searches I had never thought to tap the one source that was the most accessible and as my gaze turned towards WWII it became so obvious I felt ashamed at not pursuing it before. It simply never occurred to me to ask "What did you do in the war dad?". I suppose you don't readily accept that your own parents could be an integral part of your interests, but an answer of "Oh, I had a very uneventful war" was probably the most effective response he could have given. "Really?" I thought, "lets just see".

Persistence revealed more than I could have imagined. A few faded pictures, a couple of souvenirs that had stood the test of time, some written memoirs backed by prompted recollections and a little independent research, told me differently.

The benefits of a reserved occupation may have meant a late entry to the war for this particular soldier, but when the call did come it coincided with the preparations for the greatest sea invasion ever, leading to a further twelve months of hard fighting which would ask much of the personnel involved.

To those of us who have never experienced armed conflict, no amount of pictures, writings or tales can ever really explain what it was like. Only actual personal experience can do that. But they can give us a better idea of what happened at the sharp end and how people coped with situations alien to a 'normal' life as we would understand it. What follows, therefore, is a collection of actual events that have been related in chronological order, to set them in context with the larger picture. They are all true and they all happened to one ordinary soldier of His Majesty's forces in Europe. In truth though, many of them could have happened at almost any stage of the 1939-45 conflict and to just about any soldier of any army. They are not particularly unique. Some are quite funny, others sad. But all are examples of the ordinary man's lot in war.

This was my Dad's war.

CHAPTER 1 - FROM BLUE TO KHAKI

Eleven a.m., Sunday the 3rd September 1939 and War is declared against Germany for the second time in a quarter of a century. The young John Cropper was to be found serving as a probationary Policeman in Milnrow, Lancashire on the edge of the Pennine belt. Situated between Rochdale and Oldham, it had a small population which was mainly employed by the local mills in the cloth industry.

In addition to normal duties, the declaration of hostilities meant that John soon found the much abused saying of 'Ask a Policeman', a feature of the old Music Hall song, was on everybody's lips. "What day do I collect my gas mask?", "Where is the nearest shelter?", "When will I get ...", "How do I go about ..." and so on. He also suddenly found himself in charge of a number of rather ageing police reservists, known as the Auxiliary Police War Reserve or P.W.R.s[1], who had been called up to handle the increasing workloads. A responsibility never considered in probationary training.

Indeed, the outbreak of war occasioned the need for a large number of people to take up the mantle of civil defence and many, both old and young, were recruited to fill the roles of Wardens, Rescue Men, Auxiliary Firemen,First Aid Parties, Ambulance Drivers and Messengers. Others became Telephonists or joined the WVS. Doctors, Nurses and Nursing Auxiliaries manned First Aid Posts. It was an intense time for all but curiously, whilst the roles of all of the above were fairly well defined, that of the 'bobby' was more theoretical than actually happened in practice.

The Police were on the streets all the time, consequently they were often first on the scene. There was nothing the Policeman didn't do. He reported incidents and mustered the services, just as the Wardens were trained to do. He cleared the houses when unexploded bombs were near and moved people from shelters if they were also threatened. If he came across those trapped by debris, he became a Rescue Man and fought to free the incumbent. If they were injured he administered first aid.

When incendiaries fell he helped to put them out, but if the blaze was too great he summoned the fire brigade. If all the pump crews were out though he could gather wardens, rescue workers or anyone available, borrow appliances and attend to the job himself.

And when the dangers had passed, or even when they were still very much in evidence, it was the Policeman who guarded against looters, who dealt with the unfortunate task of recording the deaths and notifying relatives, whilst all the time performing the traditional role - that of guardian of law and order.

All exciting stuff for a young lad of 21 far from his hometown of Liverpool.

Of course Milnrow was a mere pimple on the map of England at that time and not a high risk area by any stretch of the imagination. But it was subject, nonetheless, to the same aspects of 'war fever' that gripped the rest of the country. The village soon began to have its fair share of false air raid alarms and, as could be expected, the majority happened in the small hours and were the regular cause of the young Constable's many sleepless nights.

The mayor's parade, Dale Street, Milnrow -1938. John is the first man behind Sergeant McGinty, in the foreground. The other Sergeant is Sgt. Baker and the Inspector, Mr McKie

Long before the days of portable radios and a telephone in every house, contact between the beat copper and his station was either via the good old blue Police telephone box or through a convenient public telephone. In the case of the Milnrow 'patch' it was the latter and the noise of the siren always occasioned a trip to the nearest public box.

The first real taste of 'action' occurred shortly after the formation of the L.D.V. in May 1940. Aroused from his slumbers by the now ubiquitous air raid sirens at 1.30 in the morning, a half-asleep and hastily dressed Constable Cropper stumbled down to the local phone box to report in and receive instructions. On this occasion he learned that an unidentified man ("a parachutist or spy") had been detained by the local L.D.V. platoon and he was to investigate.

A short walk of some half-mile brought him to Boundry Mill whereupon;

"........ I entered the dusty, warm, hazy atmosphere of the fire-hole through the black-out airlock and there, under the light of a single electric light bulb, sat a more than disgruntled citizen surrounded by his captors in varying styles of mufti, all wielding broomsticks or mock wooden rifles. Charlie Stott [Chairman of the Bench and local L.D.V. commander] remained somewhat in the background. On the table, amidst a variety of pint pots containing small amounts of liquid and tea-leaves, lay a gleaming brand-new A.R.P. badge. I looked at the man, who could only be distinguished from his captors by the fact that he was the only one without a band round his left arm bearing the legend 'L.D.V.'

"Have you got your identity card?" I asked, just to clear the decks.

"Ah've getten one," he said, "bur it's awhom. I just forgetten to pur it in mi pocket when I come aht, that's aw."

"I see. What's your name?" He told me. "Where do you live?" He told me that too. I turned to the company generally, "Do any of you know the street?"

"Oh, aye" they chorused.

"Well can one of you go to the house and check who lives there?"

"No need," said more than one of them, whilst yet another added, "He does."

"Do you know him?" I asked in amazement.

Oh aye," they chorused [yet again] and one added, he lives three doors from me." It turned out that they had all known each other all their lives and all were decent respectable citizens. I immediately told the man he was free to go the moment he wanted to and explained to the others the 'practical' purpose of identity cards. I pointed to the A.R.P. badge on the table. "Whose is this?"

"It's his."

"Aren't you going to take it?" I asked him.

"Nay," he said, "Ahm not. I've finished wi' it after this. Ahm 'avin' nowt no more to do wi't' war.".…"

Many years later, and strictly by chance, the Cropper family moved back to the area when John retired from the Police force in the 1970's and became a Publican at 'The Lower Bird in Hand' in Newhey - the next village along from Milnrow but still a part of John's old patch. Casual conversation with some of the older occupants of the tap room subsequently confirmed that the gentleman in question apparently kept to his word!

Very shortly after the events at Boundry Mill came a transfer to Preston;

"16 June 1940 - Transferred to H/Q Fingerprint Dept - fame and progress at last. Out in the country, little danger of being bombed here - if they have a job to reach Manchester it's even less likely they'll reach Preston. Inevitably, where danger is less, precautions are greater. We take sandwiches for lunch and tea and firewatch all night. The office is never locked or abandoned. We guard it - and the highly important criminal records."

It was a widely held belief at the time that the might of the German Luftwaffe could not reach the west coast of England, as they could never get over the Pennines. However, on the 27th June John and his colleagues were disturbed by the noise of an aircraft. They went outside for a proper look;

"..... [it was] in the distance ..... four or five miles away? We shaded our eyes with our hands and tried to determine its nationality. We had all learned a little about aircraft recognition. There were charts everywhere showing front, side and underneath silhouettes with descriptions of special features to look for. This one was flying right to left across our field of vision and in spite of the study we had made of the charts, defied recognition[2].

Slowly it went into a shallow dive and then suddenly swept up in a climb. I thought I got a fleeting glimpse of something leave it as it began its upward sweep. "That dropped something", I said ..... . The plane swept round and then we heard the 'crump'. Twice more the plane repeated its action, but we only heard one more 'crump'."

Three bombs landed in a field at Leyland but only two exploded. Whilst they were to be the only bombs dropped in the Preston area during the whole war, it appeared that the Pennines were not going to prove as much of a problem to the Nazi war machine as had at first been thought.

During the next month more tentative raids were made in the Liverpool area and by the end of August, air-raids were becoming a common occurrence. This coincided with yet another transfer, to Seaforth (Liverpool) and the war proper. At least as far as the civilian front was concerned. John's initial reaction was not promising though;

"..... First impression not appealing. Begrimed buildings, bomb damage, black shuttered windows, probably with no glass behind them, windows with glass bearing strips of sticky paper in the form of a St. George's cross over which was superimposed a St. Andrew's cross ..... not just the windows of business premises, but all, each and every one, down to the one in the 'littlest' room - and behind every one, sombre black curtains hung, or black shutters suspended ..... . No need to enforce black-out regulations here."

His journal entries for the period chart the trials that the Blitz caused for the civilian population and also some of the unusual sights it created. From the changing face of town life;

"Rows and rows of houses irreparably damaged, the occupants, lord knows where, maimed in hospital, dead, or fled, or perhaps in some cases still buried under the rubble ....."

To the mental images they evoked as the young Copper walked through the streets;

> "..... I marvelled at the effects of blast and paused before one house - one of a pair of semi- detached's which had been literally blasted away. The dividing wall still stood. High up in a little corner formed by a small piece of adjoining wall that also remained, proudly displayed, was a lavatory pan complete with plumbing, cistern and chain. Of all the places in the house to be when the bomb struck, that was the only safe place.
>
> I tried to imagine the quandary in which the occupant would have been placed had that been his position at the time the rest of the house collapsed. His small embarrassment would have outweighed that of the anticipation of the next bomb, or the sufferings of the victims of the first. To be sitting there, with his trousers down in full view, like a child on a potty. Not enough floor on which to stand to adjust his trousers, too dangerous to leap down to the rubble below, and the blast having blown all the toilet paper away.
>
> I imagined him having to wait until somebody noticed him, and when noticed, waving shyly back in answer to calls from below and then sitting patiently waiting for the fire service to put up a ladder whilst the eager crowd, gathering below to witness his rescue, shouted words of encouragement to him. Any attempt he made to adjust his dress would send showers of pieces of brick and plaster hurling down. What a predicament!"

It is said that familiarity breeds contempt or, if not contempt then a hardening of resolve or strength to bear. How else does the Nurse deal efficiently, day after day, with the horrors of mutilation or disfigurement yet still smile at all the patients and present a cheery and positive air? The same is doubtless true of all who are exposed to stressful situations time and again.

John's diary entries became progressively shorter as the business of war on a civilian population increased. During 1941 the Liverpool area suffered terribly, particularly during the first few days of May, but by August things had become fairly quiet again;

".... Picked up the paper from the mat [this morning]. The front page headlines read "97 GERMAN BOMBERS SHOT DOWN" then, in smaller type underneath "20 of our aircraft fail to return". I open the paper. The pocket cartoon depicts a theatre sister and nurse behind a post-operation trolley of laid-out instruments. The caption reads " ..... and from all these operations fourteen pairs of scissors are missing." I laugh. C'est la guerre."

There was no disrespect, no jokes at the misfortune of others, he had simply learned how to cope.

NOTES:

[1] Police War Reserve

[2] No official record of the type of aircraft can be found but it was most probably a Dornier Do17 bomber. These were used extensively over Britain and the Liverpool area in particular, one being brought down nearly a month later close to Liverpool on a similar raid.

PC 1189, John Cropper - taken shortly after his posting to Milnrow in 1938

CHAPTER 2 - PRACTICE MAKES PERFECT

Eventually allowed to volunteer for active service in July 1943, John soon found himself at No. 15 Primary Training Centre, Fulford Barracks, York, for basic infantry training with B Company, the Kings Own Yorkshire Light Infantry and an "interesting ..." 3 months. It is here that he learned the rudiments of military life including the basic elements of any soldier's routine - drilling, cleaning and marching. The latter proving a particularly difficult task, unusually so as he was already used to the disciplines of drill and marching with the Police force.

The reason? The light infantry march is noticeably faster than any other at 160 paces per minute which is suited better, perhaps, to those of slightly smaller stature who have not had the slower pace of 120 paces per minute already drummed into them. For the six foot ex-copper this single task proved the most difficult to master but after much trial and tribulation he finally got the hang of it. Following a posting to the Royal Armoured Corps though, all the hard work eventually came to nothing.

Before leaving Fulford, B Company were treated to a farewell concert. It was the standard type of amateur show with magicians, dance routines, recitations and singing;

> "There was an ATS girl who was, I am told, a bit of an Officers' blanket. Anyway it appeared that she always sang "When you wore a tulip". I don't know if it was her alleged reputation or not, but that is the only act I remember."

Maybe this first exposure to a concert party had a greater effect than he realised. In later life, John, too, was to take to the amateur stage and it would become a major feature of his retirement years.

For armoured vehicle training he was sent to the Tank training depot at Bovington, to join Squad 15A of D Company, the 52nd Tank Training Regiment. Here he was to learn the skills of a Radio Operator/Driver and receive a new cap badge in place of the bugle horn of the Kings Own Yorkshire Light Infantry - the mailed fist of the Royal Armoured Corps;

"It was one of those horrible plastic ones. I wasn't at all impressed with it so I bought a metal one from a shop in town at the first opportunity and threw the plastic one away. Lots of chaps did."

Which probably explains why the price of the utility badges made from bakelite (plastic) fetch such high prices today. He also had a change in title. Instead of the Army rank of 'Private', he now became a cavalry 'Trooper'.

Shortly after arriving all the new men were paraded for drill and off they set, some at 120 paces a minute and some at 160.

"It was like something out of a Keystone Cops movie, the Sergeant Major was getting more and more annoyed as we 'light infantry' men kept pulling away and then had to be restrained. After all that effort learning to march at a quick pace I simply couldn't march at the slower rate anymore."

Being a generally intense period, he wrote little of that time and many of his recollections of camp life are now mingled together. All, that is but one very vivid memory which, for some reason, seems as clear as ever.

A permanent base, Bovington featured a large number of ancillary staff and was blessed with the services of the ATS for the catering. Now this could be thought of as quite an advantage, especially bearing in mind the way in which the Army usually posted men to their respective units - leading to qualified people in one trade having to learn another skill because the Army insisted in employing them different roles. At least there was a better chance of the women of that time being able to cook.

It was roughly half way through the training programme and it had fallen upon John's intake to stand all guard duties as the instruction staff were away for the weekend. The men were all sleeping and living in a row of Nissan huts set out under some trees close to the perimeter. There were about 8 huts in all with the last two being the ablutions and toilet blocks, and they were occupied by about 180 men.

"It was late into the night and I was sleeping in my bunk when I awoke with a rotten stomach ache. It was cold outside and a long walk to the toilet block so I kept putting off the trip, but after a while I simply had to go so I jumped down, threw my greatcoat over my shoulders, slipped on my boots and set off.

As I made my way through the darkness I became aware of men coming slowly back towards me and others moving swiftly in the same direction. In fact there were people everywhere and I couldn't make any sense of it, not at that time of night.

Anyway, I finally reached the toilets and then found that most of the stalls were either occupied or devoid of paper, but luckily I found a vacant one near the end and settled down to almost instant relief. It was then that I began to realise that I wasn't the only sufferer of stomach ache as I heard the stamping of running feet outside accompanied by curses at the lack of paper or impatience at finding all the stalls occupied. Indeed the air was blue with curses and pleas for people to hurry up.

By the time I was on my way back virtually all the men were up, there were bodies everywhere, mainly rushing towards the toilets. It was a long night!"

Naturally the men blamed the ATS for trying to poison them, amidst rumours of some unrequited love or similar entanglement, but the reality proved to be one of the square pegs in round holes variety after all. It transpired that during the previous day a faulty water boiler had been stripped down and cleaned by the cooks, who were fed up with having to manage without it. But the cleaning agent had not been flushed out properly. Consequently the evening mugs of tea contained more ingredients than normal.

Isn't it funny what sticks in the mind?

In terms of training though, some important lessons were learned.

For radio communication, a Sherman tank operated three different systems, referred to as 'nets' after the term used for tuning a radio to the correct frequency. These were A, B and intercom. The main difference between the three being who can hear when you speak. 'A' worked on the basis of being available both to all crew members and other operators on the same frequency, was used for communication within the Squadron and had the longest range at about 25 miles. 'B' differed by only being accessible by the tank commanders in each crew, was used for communication within the Troop and had a shorter range of just 3 or 4 miles. The intercom was purely for communication within the tank itself and it was the responsibility of each individual Commander to switch the radio to the appropriate 'net' as necessary.

As could be expected though, this did not always happen quite as smoothly as it should - as the following shows:

It had been a fairly normal day for the men of the Squadron. They had driven[1] in convoy down to the ranges in the morning, spent the day there blasting away at old tank hulls and wooden mock-ups, and were now on their way back to camp, again in convoy.

The Squadron Leader was sitting out of his hatch surveying all about him and suddenly he became conscious that all the tanks were following, turrets pointing forward and guns steady in parade ground fashion. Never one to miss an opportunity he switched to 'A' and ordered "All stations, exercise your Gunners".

Now this was a fairly straightforward drill and involved the individual tank commanders picking a target, specifying the type of shell required, estimating the range and ordering the gun to traverse. Then the gun would be steadied to fire, following which the whole procedure was followed again. Of course from the casual observer's point of view you simply saw a turret revolving and the gun moving up and down. Indeed;

> "What used to happen was that the Gunner was told to swing his gun around and no actual drill was done."

Not surprisingly, therefore;

> "..... a rather tired Sergeant [commander], whose tank was a little way behind the leader, said through his 'mike' "Swing the f****** gun about Joe and satisfy the old c***"."

Unfortunately he forgot to switch the 'net' from 'A' to intercom and this rather unorthodox command was relayed around the Squadron. The next morning the Squadron boasted one newly created Trooper in its ranks, but at the cost of one rather careless Sergeant. In action though, forgetting to switch 'nets' could have more serious consequences as John was to learn a few months later.

"... rides along the cart tracks...". Evidence of early proficiency on a motorbike at Cherry Tree Farm. John is sat at the back with Sam Brown in the middle and Tommy Appleton at the controls.

Curiously, although the tanks were equipped with range finders, by the time John found himself in the Commander's seat a little later;

> "..... we weren't shown in training how they worked and I couldn't make head or tail of it. I never tried to use one, all my ranging was done by sight estimates only."

He was taught basic gunnery, though;

> "I sat leaning into a frame, similar to the type you got on anti-aircraft guns on ships, like Oerlikon cannons. This was used to control the aim and the attached gun fired small ball bearings - just like an air rifle.
>
> For targets there were cut-out shapes on a sand table to aim at and little flickering lights, indicating return fire."

And despite having learned to drive whilst with the Police, he was also given driving lessons;

> "We used to get a vehicle and then go out in groups, taking turns to drive. As I could drive already though, I spent most of my time as a passenger.
>
> They had all types of vehicles, from Daimler Scout Cars to three ton trucks and I did have a go of sorts in all of them but the day I did enjoy was when we took out a Lloyd Carrier and a Universal Carrier for a days training.

The Universal Carrier was steered by sticks and when I got my go in the afternoon it was by far the best time I had spent in the army to date - I did enjoy myself. I really made the bloody thing move, tearing around the countryside down lanes and across fields."

Indeed, he impressed the Instructor so much with his prowess that he was recommended for an instructor's post himself. The imminent need for fighting troops was greater though and he was soon to find himself posted, but not before one final driving experience;

"They also taught us to drive motorcycles, but before we started training we were split into two groups - those who had ridden before and those who had not. When they asked who had been on a bike I put my hand up, although my total experience only amounted to a few rides along the cart tracks on the farm near home.

This was deemed sufficient to advance me to the 'expert' class and I was given a bike and told to get on with it. It was a Matchless, with a foot change, but unlike the bike I had ridden at home it didn't have a little mark to show where neutral was and could I find it? Could I hell.

When they all set off on the ride from camp I was left behind still trying to set off without stalling. In the end I put it in gear and set off running with it until it kicked in and then jumped on and tore off like the clappers to try and catch up. I had no idea of where they had gone but more by luck than judgement I reached them a few miles away just as they were finishing their break and returning to camp.

In a way it was lucky, all I had to do was drive the bike in a circle and tag on the end - no need to stop and try to find neutral!"

Back at camp he was now a 'qualified' driver and, training complete, it was then on to the XXIVth Lancers, who were based at Milford on Sea preparing for the forthcoming invasion of Europe.

It was now May 1944.

NOTES:
[1] In military parlance, tanks moving in convoy were actually referred to as 'marching' - just as infantrymen did.

CHAPTER 3 - AND SO TO WAR

The XXIVth Lancers had only been formed in December 1940 as one of the six new armoured Regiments raised for the duration of the war. They had recently completed a long period of training at various locations around Britain, including the Whitby moors, Sussex Downs, Yorkshire Wolds and Cambridgeshire fens and were destined, although the young John did not know, to be one of the Invasion units earmarked for heavy casualties. They were mainly equipped with Mk III and Mk IVc (Mayfly) Sherman Tanks and were scheduled to land on Gold beach at Arromanches on D-Day itself, as armoured reserve.

By this late stage their preparation consisted mainly of vehicle maintenance and waterproofing of armoured vehicles ready for operation Overlord, the invasion of Europe. Extra manpower had been drafted in to complete these tasks in time and John, therefore, found himself a crewman without a crew, an extra pair of hands in the rush to complete preparations. He applied himself accordingly.

On the 15th May the Regiment moved to Larkhill and a few days later, on the 18th, the surplus manpower moved to camp 13 at Hursley. Here John became a reinforcement in the 8th Armoured Brigade's Forward Delivery Squadron (No.265), whose task it was to provide replacement vehicles and crews to counter losses in action.

As would be expected, with the closeness of the invasion date all troops were confined to barracks and no leave was permitted. However, it appears that these strict regulations were not maintained that rigorously as the appearance of a WREN at the gate accompanied by a Royal Artillery Captain [1], secured his release for a few hours. Long enough for the three of them to have a good meal at any rate. A few months later the WREN, May Phillips, was to become Mrs Cropper - but that is another story altogether.

By this route he eventually found himself in an M3 Honey on 10th June 1944, D-Day+4, on board an LST (Landing Ship Tank) finally heading towards France.

He had originally boarded the vessel during the morning of D-Day from the Hards at Gosport and had spent the intervening days sitting on board waiting to cross, due to a combination of storms in the Channel and crowding on the landing beaches. In the meantime his regiment had crossed from Southampton water on D-Day itself, but had ended up sitting offshore due to the same bad weather and congestion. Entering the fray on the 7th, however, they quickly found themselves in the thick of the action when they formed the left flank of the breakout from the beach-head.

May Phillips and her friend, Ella Krant, pose with a 'borrowed' bicycle at Fort Southwark April 1944

For John though, the 4 days confined to a small craft, anchored in the Solent were filled with boredom.

> "There was just the one deck and we had been loaded nose to tail, two vehicles abreast. As I was the Radio Operator there was nothing to do. One of the other crewmen was called Keith Cornish, and he was an ex- public schoolboy who had once been sent for Officer training but who considered himself totally unsuited for the role and had said so. As a consequence he had been 'returned to unit'. He was to be recommended again for a Commission a few months after landing in France - but would turn it down again.
>
> Some of the chaps spent the time gambling but as neither Keith nor I were gamblers we didn't join in and spent much of the time chatting. Others just sat around, lost in their own thoughts."

John had been asked by the Bos'n of the L.S.T. to paint the Regimental badge (crossed lances with the letters 'XXIV' across them, set in a circle with the words 'LANCERS' surmounted by a king's crown) on the wheelhouse fairing alongside those of the other units he had carried, both in the months of training preceding the invasion and on the monumental day itself. In the boredom of being on board waiting for the crossing to commence this delicate operation helped to pass the time.

Inevitably this meant that he and the Bos'n started chatting as well, discussing their various trades, the war, the invasion and so on. Indeed, in the scheme of things they became quite friendly which ultimately led to a rather detailed lesson on how to steer the LST.

As a reward for the new paint job, and in view of his interest, John was allowed to steer the vessel for a while once the crossing began. He had been taught that the spokes on the ships wheel represented degrees on the compass, thus allowing the helmsman to respond quickly to commands for changes in course. Unfortunately though, lack of any real practice meant that the wheel had to be returned after a very short time, but at least he had acquired enough experience of steering a boat to be able to take his youngest son on the rowing boats at Heaton Park near Manchester many years after. Or so he later claimed during one of those lazy summers of the writer's youth, shortly before the motor cut out and a tow had to be begged from a passing row boat!

Standing by the Bos'n for the rest of the crossing, there followed an interesting chat with this new found friend.

It transpired that one of the earlier units the Bos'n ferried was an American one who, in the Bos'n's words "Knew everything". Such was the annoyance caused by these passengers that when the craft came to discharging its troop of Shermans;

> " ..... the Bos'n halted some 10 yards out saying that he could get no further in. The first tank accelerated out, hit the water and progressed at a rapid rate, down. It sank out of sight! I realised then that you should always be friendly with your transport crew and hoped that it wouldn't happen to me."

Trooper Cropper had made a mental note and he silently thought to himself, "Better not upset this bugger or I'm for it.". Clearly he didn't as he was landed safely on Gold beach at Arromanches later that same day without even getting his tracks wet.

His most vivid memory of the landing though was;

> "During the trip across, all you could see as far as every horizon was a vast armada of ships, all sailing in ordered lines towards France ..... just as we were moving towards land we passed close to a Battleship, the Ramilles I think, and it was pouring fire into some unseen target beyond the shore. It was an incredible sight and I though "Welcome to the real war"..... ."

Just as could be expected, in the midst of the greatest seaborne invasion ever the well laid plans of the Forward Delivery Squadron to supply either replacement tanks or complete crews went by the board and 3 days later he was off to his Regiment as an individual replacement for a man lost in action. Quite a blessing really as life with the FDS was not exactly pleasant for the men;

> "They treated you like cattle ..... the food was appalling and I detested it."

It seems that this was not an isolated experience either as John had occasion to pass through the FDS more than once over the coming months - but by then he had learned how to make his stay as short as possible. The individual Regiments were fiercely loyal to 'their' men and despite the principal of the FDS supplying only full crews it wasn't uncommon for men on arrival to;

> " ..... simply ring up the Sergeant Major at [the] Regiment and he'd say "Right - there will be a truck there for you in a couple of hours"."

Indeed;

> "They would even send a 3 tonner if a jeep wasn't available [even if it was] just for one man"

On this occasion it took a couple of days to get wise to the procedure but when he finally did get to a telephone;

> "I wasn't on the phone 10 seconds, just long enough to give my name and say where I was, when I was told, "Right - I'll send a truck for you - you'll be back this evening" ..... and I was."

Later in the war he was to receive calls from his own ex- crewmen stuck at the FDS, many of the tank commanders did, and they too were brought back as quickly as possible into the fold of the Regiment.

On the 14 June 1944 John Cropper finally joined the fighting war and became Radio Operator on B Baker of 4 Troop, "B" Squadron, XXIVth Lancers, 8th Independent Armoured Brigade. A 75mm gunned M4A2, diesel engined Sherman called 'Pin-Up Girl', commanded by a Corporal who had been in action since the Regiment landed on the 7th. At that time the rest of the crew was made up by Troopers A S 'Ritchie' Richardson (driver), T H Tutin (co-driver) and Fred Gasson (gunner).

For the next 3 weeks he was to become an active participant in the actions fought around the villages of Cristot, Parc de Bois Londe, St Pierre, Tessel Wood, Villers Bocage, Rauray and Hottot. But not entirely in the role he had trained for.

Captain Webster - taken the day after the ceasefire.
5 May 1945

NOTES:

[1] Captain F Webster RA

CHAPTER 4 - PROMOTION

For a tank crew in action there are a number of lessons quickly learned that can make the difference between survival or a potentially horrible end. The effects of being in a brewed up tank were well known by all crews, certainly those within the XXIVth Lancers. It was a fear that all held but one that was kept out of conscious thought because, if dwelt upon, the fear could take over. On occasion it did.

It was not for nothing the Sherman crews name for their tanks was 'Ronson Lighters', or 'Ronsons', echoing that company's claim that their cigarette lighters lit first time. Even the Germans called them 'tommy cookers' as they would invariably catch fire if hit, giving the crew a mere 20 seconds at best to evacuate the metal box.

The 5 crew members in the body of an M4A2 Sherman have 3 basic ways of getting out[1]. 2 of these are hatches in the front, above the Driver and Co-Driver and even unhindered it can easily take 10 or 12 seconds for those two occupants to squeeze out. This gives precious little time for the Gunner and Radio Operator sitting within the confines of the rapidly heating metal coffin to use either of these routes, which in reality are extremely difficult for them to access anyway. The 3rd exit is up through the commander's hatch, through which all the crew can evacuate if there is sufficient time.

*During a pause in the march.
"the first thing was to get a brew going".*

Remember though, that the inside of a tank is very cramped with little room for an individual to manoeuvre. Just think how difficult it is to squeeze from the driver's seat to the passenger seat in a modern car - and then multiply that 100 times.

If the turret hatch was closed, however, the simple fact was that in the event of the tank being hit, the confines of the interior coupled with the highly restricted area for personal movement usually meant that the Gunner and Radio Operator didn't leave. Even if the Commander did not encounter a welded hatch caused by the heat of the armour piercing shell, the time taken to force it open and then get himself out left little change from 20 seconds. Certainly;

> "..... the Radio Operator was in such a tight spot that his chances of getting out after being brewed-up were virtually nil."

As a result, most crews never closed the turret lid simply because;

> "..... the damn things were so heavy and the chance of something coming through the top was minimal".

It was not simply a matter of climbing up through the hatch though. This escape route could only be used by the Driver and Co-Driver if the turret ring was positioned with the gun pointing in the right direction, roughly 45° to the left or right of centre, otherwise that exit was effectively blocked off from the body of the tank by the moving cage below the turret. Even given that this is positioned with the gaps in the right place thus allowing those crew members access, the breech of the gun still formed a major obstacle for the Operator who was seated in a very tight spot within the cage itself, but on the wrong side from the open hatch.

Given that all these factors are favourable, if the Commander or Gunner had been injured or killed when the tank was hit, then the exit would be virtually blocked by the body. It is with little surprise, therefore, that casualties amongst tank crews were high.

If you have ever wondered why photographs of tanks in action frequently show personal gear stowed at the rear when it seemed obvious that the risk of losing it was fairly high, then here is the reason why.

To begin with, there was some spare room inside but only a little as most of the spare space was taken up with ammunition. The Sherman was a fighting machine first and foremost and not designed for living in, so if personal equipment had to be brought inside and the tank was hit then there would be a high risk of this equipment jolting loose and jamming the rotating gear, preventing the turret from being turned to the optimum position for escape. Whether there would be enough time to rotate the turret is another matter.

> "You could always replace your kit, and it was worth the risk for the piece of mind. Anyway, with the bedding packed down over the engine it guaranteed that it was always warm when you got the chance to use it!"

The 5th crew member, the Commander, was the eyes of a Sherman and in order to perform this function he sat with his head poked up above the turret hatch when in action. Without those eyes the tank was in grave risk of attack from infantry and could easily miss the approach of enemy armour, due to the limited view through the observation slits. Indeed, the tank was effectively blind when relying on the observation slits alone.

For the Commander there was always the additional fear of being hit by a sniper's bullet because of this exposure and, as an expedient, he would dip his head up and down quickly when in heavy action, in order to lessen the chance of this happening;

> "It was no secret to the German troops that allied tanks were not over-crewed and that the removal of one crew member could make the vehicle ineffective."

Consequently it did not take much intelligence to realise that the chap with his head stuck out of the turret was the easy option to disable the tank and he invariably drew a great deal of small arms fire when in close combat. One unit lost 42 Commanders[2] alone in the few days fighting following D-Day and for the month of June the XXIVth suffered 27 Officer and 115 other rank casualties, losing 38 tanks in the process.

Inevitably this put an additional strain on every Commander and such was the case with the Corporal of B Baker. His obvious discomfort showed when he began to sit with his head down for longer and longer periods, until the whole crew became very edgy indeed. After a small confab with his three comrades John asked if he could 'have a go..' in the Commander's seat during one action. The Corporal was most agreeable;

> "It reached the stage when we would set out from a laager with him sitting up top and me in the Radio Operator's chair. Then as we came closer to the action, we would change places and I wouldn't return to my seat until we were well on our way back .... When you think about it, he was probably putting himself in the worst possible place to be in if the tank was hit. For my part, I felt I'd got by far the best end of the trade."

As any true student of war knows, battle fatigue (referred to by the soldiers as going "bomb happy") is as much of an injury as a bullet in the leg. Eventually, the Corporal came to accept that he was a liability in his current state and reported sick. Very shortly afterwards John was summoned to the Squadron Leader's tank and after a brief meeting with the Squadron Leader he found himself promoted to Acting Corporal with very little ceremony. He was then presented with one set of Corporal's stripes which were duly sewn on the left sleeve of his greatcoat. It was to be a considerable time before he could boast a set on each arm.

Later that day a replacement Operator arrived, John's colleague from the crossing - Keith Cornish. The crew was once again complete.

Since landing, the tanks had progressively taken on more of the appearance of their surroundings in an attempt to give them a slight edge against German observers. Acquiring much of the local foliage in the process;

> "We stuck wire netting and allsorts around the tank just to break up the outline. Bits of twig, branches, clumps of greenery, in fact whatever came to hand.
>
> In particular, we used parachute silk when we could get it. The parachutists used to drop on camouflaged silk whilst the supplies were dropped on coloured ones, red, yellow and so on, representing whatever they carried. When we got our hands on the camouflaged ones we draped them over the tank. At times you couldn't recognise her."

They also quickly acquired another skill;

"Whenever we stopped the first thing was to get a brew going. You wouldn't always get the chance to drink it and quite often we would move off again before it was ready, but it was always the first thing we did.

If we were gagging for a drink and had to move off, then someone would sit on the back whilst it boiled up or we would pass it down inside and the co-driver would finish it off on the camp stove, which he stood on the floor between his legs. We had to have our brew."

The XXIVth had been in action since John joined them, mainly;

"..... standing in hedges and belting away at anything that moved or looked like moving..",

but as the immediate job of the British forces on this front was to form a 'hinge', against which the might of the German army was to be drawn whilst the American forces broke out from their beach-head, the hedges he stood in were many and varied;

"As we moved the tanks backwards and forwards along the roads there was one danger I don't think anyone had anticipated.

The signals boys had laid lots of telephone communication wires all around and to stop them being cut by vehicles going across they were suspended on poles over the roads and tracks - at about turret height. We were always running into them and they would break because they'd catch under the open turret lid and snap - 'Signals' were always complaining.

On one occasion we were crossing a cornfield. The corn was a good three feet high against the side of the tank as we pressed on through and I was watching it sway as we pushed it aside. Anyway, we ran into a wire which hit the turret lid but instead of catching, it flipped over the top.

Within an instant it caught me in the throat and I was nearly throttled. I had to fling myself out of the turret on my back and force myself flat whilst using my forearms to keep the wire off my neck and face. It was a close one."

Constant manoeuvring brought other dangers as well;

"There was a time a little later in the campaign[3] when we used to move the tanks along the line at night quietly, or as quietly as a tank could move, to try and deceive the Germans into thinking we had more armour than we really did. The way it happened was that we would be led by a Dingo with a small red light hanging down at the back - that was all we could see to follow and you had to be directly behind it to see that. The tanks further back in the column had a very hard time of it.

Well, we were moving along one night and I had lost sight of the tank in front. As I strained to see through the dark I caught sight of a red light a little to my right and ordered the driver to "apply right stick", to turn us towards it - he wouldn't have been able to see anything from his position and relied entirely on my directions. Just as I ordered "stick off" we pitched over the edge of a bank and were moving along, tilted at a very dangerous angle to the right.

My first thought when we jerked sideways was that the tank may roll and I would find myself crushed, as I was stood with my head and shoulders out of the turret. So I ordered the driver to steer into it and we ploughed on down, taking at least one tree with us on the way. After a short time we levelled out and then started climbing again, eventually getting back on hard ground.

The column must have been moving around the rim of a saucer-like crater and I had cut across the middle by mistake."

"B" Squadron had its share of set-piece actions as well, notably at Parc de Bois Londe just a few days after John had arrived on the 17th June, when they were used to dislodge enemy infantry and tanks. During July much of the action was in the vicinity of another wood, Tessel wood, close by. It was an intense time and mistakes did happen;

"The German Spandau machine gun made a very distinctive sound, easily distinguishable from our own Bren. Anyway there was a period when all the soldiers, ours and theirs, were mixed up with each other. You were never sure quite how close or in what direction Gerry was.

Consequently we were firing on whatever targets presented themselves and when we heard Spandau fire in a wood opposite we sent over some H.E.

I learned later that the Spandaus had been captured by some of our own troops who had been using them when we opened fire."

It was also here that;

"We were down to one Officer as all the others had either been killed or wounded. A Lieutenant was leading what was left of our Squadron in an extended line and you could hardly see anything because of the damn bocage[4]. He decided to push into a little wood and explore it.

Over the 'net' came instructions to 2 Able to cover him, quickly amended to an order to follow him in. The Commander of 2 Able forgot to switch to intercom and the next thing heard on 'net' was "Driver left, driver left", followed by.. "But he's gone right Sergeant?" and the reply "I know bloody well he's gone right but I'm not following that f****** c***, it's too f****** dangerous."

Casualties had been very heavy and whilst the crews accepted the risks they were not prepared to simply throw their lives away for no apparent gain. It was a time fraught with tension and to the troops on the ground there seemed little evidence of any overall plan;

"The basic tactic seemed to be 'Press on'. We constantly seemed to be just pushing forward and then pulling back to re-fuel and re-arm. The most common type of message picked up on 'net' at that time was "Press on, there's nothing in front of you ... intelligence says there's nothing there." followed by "F*** intelligence, who the hell's shooting at me if there's nothing there?". I had conversations like that on more than one occasion."

The crews had seen and experienced much since the landing and their frustration, tension and resignation to the task in hand was summed up neatly by an unknown writer in the XXIVth Lancers newsletter on the 18th July:

Six weeks ago today we sighted the French coast; and in the short time since that day we have all seen enough of the horror and beastliness of war to know that we will never tolerate this sort of thing again. And then comes the sickening thought that this is just what our fathers said.

Early on in the comprehensive planning for the invasion it was realised that certain units would take the brunt of the fighting and thus suffer heavy casualties. This same planning had made allowances for replacing the lost manpower but, perhaps inevitably, predictions fell short of actual requirements. It was arranged, therefore, that certain units would be broken up and the survivors, if any, used to re-enforce other regiments. The XXIVth were earmarked for this dubious privilege and on the 24th July a War Diary entry was made, neatly and in capital letters;

> AT 1745 HOURS THE COMMANDING OFFICER,
> LT COL W A C ANDERSON DSO INFORMED THE REGIMENT
> THAT THE 24 LANCERS WERE TO BE DISBANDED

Lancer Life, the voice of the soldiers, was a little more emotive in its appraisal:

> It is ..... impossible to put into words what everybody feels; how to convey on paper the ..... sadness in many hearts at the prospect of losing so soon and so swiftly the friends with whom we have soldiered ..... . What stories our grandchildren will hear of 'Tiger - Tiger' night! Who will ever forget Point 103? Shall we possibly one day re-visit a restored St Pierre, a new Fontenay, a free France, to pay homage to the memory of so many grand friends who have fallen on the journey? .....

A couple of days later they moved to Sully and from the 1st to 10th August the Regiment was broken up with all Officers and other ranks being posted, as far as was possible, to those Regiments they wished to go to. The XXIVth Lancers ceased to exist. Fortunately casualties had not been quite as extensive as anticipated, possibly because of the delayed landing, and as "B" Squadron's 3 and 4 Troops were still intact they volunteered to transfer en-masse. On the 4th August, therefore;

> " ..... we just changed cap badges and were issued with a couple of collar dogs each, the Lancers didn't have those, and so became Yeomanry[5]. This came about because Cowan and Cameron, the Troop Commanders, were quite pally and decided that they would try to stay together. They came up with the idea of transferring to the Sherwood Rangers so called a meeting of each Troop and put it to the vote. The main thing that swayed everyone was the fact that the SRY weren't as full of bull as some of the armoured units - and we could stay together of course."

In total, two Officers and twenty six other ranks transferred across together with their equipment[6] and John now commanded B Baker, 4 Troop, "B" Squadron, The Sherwood Ranger Yeomanry, 8th Indepenent Armoured Brigade.

Tired and very weary, the crew look to their stomachs. Having completed the "brew" (note kettle), the boiling pot is now on the fire.

NOTES:

1 In fact there was a fourth exit. Behind the Co-Driver's seat was a small escape hatch, but that was not the normal route chosen as, with-it being constantly closed and close to the muck and grime of the floor, it was usually difficult to open. Also, with it only being a short distance from the ground it was awkward to use in a hurry and once through the escapee still had to crawl from under the tank.

2 The Sherwood Rangers Yeomanry. In total, between the 6th June and 8th July in the beach-head area, the 8th Armoured Brigade lost 73 Officers and 359 other ranks, killed and wounded.

3 Whilst with the Sherwood Rangers Yeomanry during an action at Cleve in September 1944.

4 The 'Bocage' type of country was about the most unsuitable arena for an armoured operation that could be imagined. It consisted mainly of small strips of pasture land with very thick hedges, which stood higher than the tank turrets. All of this was divided by banks and ditches, intersected by sunken roads and tree flanked lanes. German snipers and anti-tank weapons could appear anywhere, even from behind as movement was covered by the terrain, so it was a particularly stressful time for tank crews and survival at times was little better than a lottery.

5 In fact the Officers of the XXIVth did wear collar badges, miniature versions of the cap badge in silver metal.

6 2 Mk IVc Mayfly's, having a crew of 4 men each, and 4 Sherman Mk III's, with a crew of 5. The personnel who transferred were: Lt A Cameron (W.I.A.), 2Lt Harry Cowan (W.I.A.), Sgt B W A Symes, A/Corp's John Cropper (W.I.A. 18.11.44), C F Lambourne, L/Corp C E Burnet (KIA 10.9.44), Trp's. L Beddow, W Blaxell (KIA 10.9.44), J Booker, Keith Cornish (KIA 19.11.44), F W J Eley (KIA 14.8.44), Frederick Gasson (KIA 19.11.44), L C Heavens (P.O.W. 12.9.44), A A Lake (KIA 11.9.44), J A MacDonald, R McFarlane, J Pelter, H Pinfold, Henry G Randle (KIA 12.9.44), A S Richardson (W.I.A. 19.11.44), E Riches, L F Robinson, A Rose (P.O.W. 12.9.44), J V Ruffell (W.I.A.), J D Simmons (KIA 22.11.44), Harry Thomas (KIA 12.9.44), T H Tutin (W.I.A. 19.11.44) and C B C Williams. The details in brackets show their fate, where known, whilst serving with the SRY.

CHAPTER 5 - A TEST OF NERVE

The SRY had been in constant action since D-Day itself and in that time had been at the forefront of the fighting, being the first troops into Bayeaux, supporting the actions on and around Point 103 and at St Pierre, together with the XXIVth Lancers, and forging forward at Fontenay, Rauray and Briquessard. Indeed they had not only been living up to 231 Brigades motto of 'Dash and Determination' but by the middle of July, Brigadier Prior- Palmer was beginning to express concern that the Regiment he considered the best trained armoured unit in that theatre of the war may soon cease to be an effective force due to the heavy casualties.

The arrival of two new 'blooded' troops was like a gift from the gods, therefore, and whilst the Regiment was pulled out of the line for a short rest at Coulvain only 4 days later, it was not before these new 'recruits' had been used in anger to support infantry attacks at Ondefontaine. This was not going to be a long rest but the services of ENSA, a cinema and, perhaps more importantly, a mobile bath unit were much appreciated. At least by those who got the chance to use them. For the men of B Squadron the time was spent with maintenance and sleep. All too soon though they were back on the move supporting the 7 Hants at Les Haies - losing 4 more tanks in the process.

The threat to tanks and their crews ever since the invasion had become more and more related to what the English termed 'bazookas' rather than to the Panthers, Tigers and tank killers of the German armoured units. The latter, though in profusion during the early weeks of the fighting, soon began to suffer the problems of fuel shortages and increasing maintenance problems. But when they were in evidence, their sheer size announced their presence and the British crews at least had a very good chance of spotting them. Bazookas, known to the Germans as the Panzerfaust, were available in large numbers, were man portable and in the undulations of the countryside or the confines of built-up areas one, unseen figure had the ability to wreak havoc on an armoured column.

Understandably, therefore, crews became anxious when they were pressing forward, even with the benefit of infantry support.

The Panzerfaust had been introduced into the German arsenal in December 1942 as the infantryman's answer to the T34 tanks they encountered on the

Russian front. This original weapon had a limited range of about 30 metres but could pierce armour plating of up to 140mm at an angle of 30° and it was light, easily portable, disposable and recoilless. By January 1943 it had already been improved to penetrate 200mm of armour, which was more than sufficient as the thickest plate on a T34 was only 45mm. On a Churchill Mk VII or VIII this was a more healthy 150mm but on the various models of Sherman, even with added plates, it was still only 100mm.

Further developments followed concentrating on improving range, so by early 1944 the Panzerfaust 60 metre model was available and this was superseded by the 100 metre model in November. As an indication of how many were available, in the month of January 1945 alone 1,200,000 were produced.

It is with no surprise, therefore, that casualties to the Panzerfaust were high and tension amongst the crews increased rapidly whenever there was a threat that they may be near.

The date was now the 16th August and "B" Squadron was detailed for an attack on the town of Berjou, which was on the other side of a bridgehead over the Noireau river recently established by elements of 214 Brigade. With the first rays of the morning sun beginning to pierce the darkness of dawn, the sound of diesel engines filled the air and the 31.5 ton monsters lumbered forward over a specially constructed tank ford. Once across, the climb was steep and via a winding road heavily wooded on either side.

The going was tough, snipers and Panzerfausts were all around. By the time they reached the top they had destroyed 8 enemy machine gun nests, but at a cost of 7 tanks damaged by those accursed anti-tank weapons - and the objective had still not fallen;

> "I kept a Sten gun and, later, a Schmeiser as well just laid on the top of the turret in case the Gerry infantry got too close. And I had my revolver, of course, a .38 Webley [Mk IV], but I was always too busy with the business of war and never did use any of them in anger. The Sten got lost along the way somewhere, it probably fell off whilst in action or when we were manoeuvring."

The loss of the STEN was not lamented though;

"They could be bloody dangerous things. If you had a full magazine in and it got a sharp jolt it was enough to chamber a round and fire.

I once saw an infantry chap jump down from the back of a 3 tonner. He had his STEN slung over his back with the barrel pointing upwards. As he landed the impact caused the bolt to bounce and the gun fired and shot the back of his head off and killed him."

Casualties were now getting critical, indeed the Regiment's Officers were beginning to fear that the Sherwood Rangers Yeomanry would go the way of the XXIVth Lancers and be disbanded. As for "B" Squadron, they had been in action all day under shell and mortar fire without replenishment and were making little progress. Despite the position though, two more squadrons joined them to try and tip the balance.

It was during this action that 4 Baker found itself pushing forward through some heavy shrubbery in the lea of a wood;

"You could hardly see in front of the tank, the damn stuff was all around us and it was frightening, Gerry could have been anywhere. Our nerves were on edge, they always were in action but more-so when you strained to hear or see.

Then all of a sudden there was a hell of a screaming roar and I frantically spun round in the turret to see what it was. Everybody was scared to death.

A German fighter passed overhead, so low I automatically ducked. It couldn't have been more than 30 or 40 feet above me hugging the contours and as it disappeared from view, another scream announced a second plane. But this time it was a British one on its tail.

As the German plane climbed back into view in the distance it was hit and disappeared again, but this time in flames"

Not an unusual event you would think, in the middle of a battle zone, but almost the straw that broke the camel's back;

"Our nerves were shot and Ritchie and Keith started an argument, over music I think. Within seconds they were literally screaming at each other - I had to be very firm with them to break it up ..... it was a long time before either of them uttered another word."

This temporary insanity did not last long, there was still a battle to fight, but the relief at not having been targeted by a Panzerfaust needed an outlet. A few months later Keith wouldn't be so lucky again.

The next day Berjou fell and they moved on to take St Honorine La Chardonne as well. By this time the danger of encirclement in the Falaise pocket forced the German high command to order a withdrawal and the crew of 4 Baker were to get a short respite;

> "For most of the time we slept in the tank, although it didn't make the comfiest of bedrooms. The Co- Driver and Driver could tilt their seats a bit to give more room and the Loader, with a bit of an effort, could curl around the base of his seat - on the floor. The Gunner's seat wasn't too bad as he had a bit of room but the Commander's seat was most uncomfy.

> Sometimes I could re-arrange 3 or 4 live rounds to sleep on but there wasn't much room and no matter how you lay, some part was always on a sharp edge of some sort. I had two small round seats, one for sitting inside the turret and the other higher up, so that I could sit with my head and shoulders out of the turret. With the top seat folded up I could sit on the bottom seat and rest my head on that, but whatever you did it was not at all pleasant. It was always very hard and very cold whatever you did."

You can imagine, therefore, that the opportunity to dismount and lie on the floor to sleep for a couple of days was most welcome.

With the retreating German army now in some disarray 21 Army Group, of which the 8th Armoured Brigade was a part, were to receive new orders from General Montgomery: To destroy the enemy in north-eastern France; clear the Pas de Calais; capture the Belgian airfields and open up the port of Antwerp. The task of pushing into Belgium fell on the Guards Armoured Division, with the 8th Armoured Brigade and 50 Division in support. The next chapter of the War was about to begin.

On the 23rd, therefore, there began an advance with a speed unmatched since 8th Army actions in the desert during 1942/43. Shortly after dawn the SRY crossed the start line and passed through Courtelles, Abbeville, Cagnes and Bailleux, sometimes at speeds that could only be described as tremendous for tanks moving across country. Indeed, during that day they had 19 tanks off the road with bogey trouble. By nightfall they had travelled 40 miles when they pulled into a Pear Orchard 3 miles east of Laigle. They were now

One of the Troop's M4A2 75mm Sherman tanks. Rob is seated in the turret and the figure on the right is Pete Taylor. From left to right the others are John, Bill Jackson, Ted King and Frank Milner. The final man has not been identified.

to wait there until the 43rd (Wessex) Division forced a crossing of the Seine at a town called Vernon a couple of days later. This delay gave them a chance to prepare for the next stage;

> "We already had a five pointed white star painted on top of the turret, but as we were progressing so quickly we were now issued with a luminous tarpaulin for aircraft recognition. That had a red star on a yellow or luminous green background and was supposed to be easier to see from the air but it was a hell of a job to attach because we had kit everywhere and it was difficult to fasten down so that it wasn't in the way of the turret. In the end we anchored it to the co-axial machine gun but as that moved when it fired it was far from satisfactory."

Not 100% effective either. Later during this same advance the armour was advancing so rapidly that they continually seemed to be in the enemy lines. An area designated as a 'free-fire' zone for the allied air support;

"We were strafed twice by allied planes, Americans, and on both passes all the cannon shells landed to our right. The planes can't have been more than 30 or 40 yards above our heads as they made their passes so the tarpaulins clearly didn't work. Not a single round landed closer than 5 yards, so I don't think the Germans were in much danger."

When they resumed the chase on the 27th passing through La Neuve Cire, Conches, Evreux and Chambray, to reach the bridgehead at Vernon sur Seine, their speed of advance had increased even further with an additional 68 miles under their belts. The 28th saw a break-out from the Seine bridgehead with a 28 mile advance and, on the next day, Acos was captured and St Remy taken with yet another 20 mile gain - for no casualties. When the tired crews pulled in to Laager at Beauvais on the 30th they now had 156 miles behind them and everything was looking good.

For John, this advance had been as much a test of reading the terrain as anything else;

"The mileage started to take its' toll on the tanks and one of the "B" Squadron Officers 'borrowed' ours, leaving us to follow on as best we could in his once the fitters had worked on it. We did a lot of track bashing[1] on that trip.

Of course, that meant we followed on alone and as we were on radio silence I had to rely wholly on the maps we were given. We were normally issued with maps of the immediate area, just enough to fit our map cases and show details for a few square miles but the advance became so rapid that I eventually ran off all the maps I had. Later on we were issued with slips of paper giving town names in order of march, instead of maps, but on this occasion I was simply left to luck

Surprisingly though I actually caught up without running into trouble, but not until I took a chance with the radio. I was about 300 yards away from the laager - not bad considering what was virtually blind navigation in the end."

On the 1st September they finally crossed the Somme at Laigle Pres Amiens and the Squadron ran into the first sign of opposition south of the village of Flesselles, where a Mk IV tank, hidden on a railway station, knocked out a Honey tank belonging to their 'Recce' troop. They pushed on regardless though, towards Nours where they engaged scattered infantry units. From there it was on to Sus St Leger and another 50 mile advance under their belts.

The vehicles were now showing more and more signs of wear so the next 24 hours were spent in long overdue maintenance. However, by the evening of the 2nd September they were back on the road once more, covering a further 24 miles. By the end of the 3rd they reached Lille and had clocked up 65 miles more. All the crews were dog tired, but the crew of 'B' Baker had a little more than exhaustion to sleep off;

"We were moving in column, with the Gerries retreating ahead of us. At one point we reached a stage when the Gerries appeared to be moving away faster than we were advancing and word reached us that they had probably pulled some troops out to our left, so that they could attack us in the flank as we passed by.

4 Troop was taken out of the column and ordered out to cover the left flank, so we moved off and formed an extended column of our own along the flank of the regiment. Well we were so spread out that you couldn't see the other tanks - what with the terrain, undergrowth, shrubbery and a distance of about 200 yards between each tank it was as though we would have to fight the war on our own if anything happened.

Just as we pulled into one spot about 20 French people suddenly appeared, cheering and shouting - and waving bottles of wine at us. This was the first time we had seen any real welcome from the French. Up until then we had been moving whenever we came into contact with them and their greetings had usually taken the form of them passing up fresh peaches to us. In fact we almost lived on peaches for a while there were so many.

Anyway, it had been raining a little during the morning, but it was warm now and all in all a very pleasant day. Keith became the interpreter, with his schoolboy French, and before you knew it all the lads had climbed down from the tank and I was left on top keeping a look out. There was a constant chance of counter-attack so we needed to be alert.

One chap had a bottle of Calvados, it was as clear as water and very drinkable. We were all taking a swig as it was passed around and Keith decided to return the gift so he fished out some cigarettes and started to offer them to the Frenchmen. When he opened up his box of matches though some fell on the floor and as he bent down to pick them up he fell flat on his face.

I thought "the beggars drunk" so decided I had better get down and sort
him out. After all we were in serious threat from Gerry. But as I tried to lift
myself out of the turret I couldn't. I was drunk too!"

Fortunately the feared counter-attack did not materialise - not that 4 Baker
would have done much to stop it if it had! The journey back to the column
was not an easy one;

"I suppose if you are going to drink and drive then a tank is probably the
best vehicle to be in. You have to actually move the sticks to change
direction so if you do nothing, then you just keep going forward. Unless
the terrain affects the speed of one of the tracks causing you to turn that
is."

*"... where there's a farm...". In this case there was a pig. Johnny Taylor, a
butcher in civilian life, makes short work of it. The pig was shared
amongst some other Squadron crews and Ron Hill, a veteran of "C"
Squadron, remembers vividly the after effects of pork washed down with
neat gin !*

The next few days saw yet another 25 mile advance and the Belgian border
was crossed. Isolated pockets of Germans began to appear, although action
was limited and once they reached the village of Rennaix there was time for
a little more maintenance. Time to prepare for what was to be one of the
Regiment's fiercest engagements.

With the onset of action though came a good example of the phrase 'an army marches on its' stomach'. Now even I, whose military career has been limited to a few exercises with the territorials, have learned one of the golden rules of survival for the ordinary soldier. If you have the opportunity to eat, take it. Who knows when the chance will come again.

I suspect that this simple expedient would be repeated by virtually every serving soldier since time began and it was certainly so with the crew of 4 Baker.

The first few days of September was a time when there was an almost constant state of alert, with frequent bouts of aggressive fire. So, to even-out pressure on the crews the Troop's took turn and turn about in the lead.

This particular day had nothing to differentiate it from any of the others, the weather was not particularly good and the enemy seemed everywhere as usual. After a morning's 'stint' at the front 4 Troop pulled over to the side of the road to allow the rest of "B" Squadron to move past, have a quick stretch and then join the rear of the column. They had barely started to draw breath when the head of the column ran into some opposition and the radio crackled to deploy;

> "We spread out into a field at the side of the road and began to form a line. Then we started to move roughly in line with the road when I spotted some farm buildings off to my left. I immediately gave the order to head for them and the Troop Leader shouted across, something like "Where the hell do you think you're going!", but I got the message. I pointed to the farm and he turned to follow, with the rest of the Troop close behind.
>
> It wasn't that it was a strategic position, or that I had seen any Gerries, but where there's a farm there are usually chickens. And where there are chickens you can usually find eggs."

The farm was quickly occupied by the men of 4 Troop, who then set to the task of rounding up the fowl for close 'interrogation' later;

> "There were people running everywhere after the birds, one chap was even trying to bring them down with a Sten gun ... he missed with every shot."

Their occupation of the farm did not go unnoticed though and very soon;

> "The Gerries put a mortar 'stonk' down on us and everyone dived for cover. One poor chap tried to crawl under our tank but was kicked out again because he had left his chicken behind and the others wouldn't let him back under until he had been back to get it."

Fortunately there were no casualties though and when they eventually pulled out;

> "Ted King[2] was still sat on the back of the tank cooking a chicken in a little pan over a camp stove. When the action started to hot up a little later he had to climb back in because he was the Gunner, so the stove, pan and chicken were passed down to the Co-Driver and as we went into action he was sat in the front of the tank with this chicken, cooking away at his feet. You'd be amazed how long it takes to boil a chicken."

Using a sten gun to kill a chicken may sound a bit like taking a sledgehammer to crack a nut but in a way, that also happened on occasion;

> "You would think that just about anything could be used to open a can of bully beef, but that's not so. I've seen people use allsorts to try and get in to a can, spanners and suchlike - one chap even tried using a sledgehammer but he didn't get in."

Whilst at Rennaix, word reached the Brigade that the Germans were to make a stand on the Albert Canal. To counter this, the Regiment was ordered to push on towards Bourg Leopold in order to gain a bridgehead. They moved out on the 9th September.

NOTES:
[1] 'Track Bashing' basically involved taking a 7lb sledge hammer to the track plates and connectors in order to re-set them after they shook loose.
[2] Ted King had joined the crew temporarily as a replacement for one of the crewmen who had been taken ill and was to re-join as a permanent crew member in 1945.

CHAPTER 6 - COUNT YOUR DEAD

Amongst my father's written memoirs is a vivid account of an action at Gheel in Belgium, between the 10th and 13th September 1944. As a military event it has probably long since passed into history, being 'just another day' in the advance to the Rhine and remembered only by the few who were there, but as an example of life at the sharp end it could describe a thousand different days for a thousand different soldiers and brings home the true face of battle.

The war diary for the SRY is unusually detailed for an action 3 days long, but it summarises with a simple sentence:

> During the past 3 days the Regiment has experienced some of the bitterest fighting since D-Day.

Bitter indeed, 11 tanks were destroyed and 2 damaged, with 2 officers and 21 other ranks being killed.

Tanks of 4 Troop pause on the march. Note the ubiquitous fire. A brew is once more under way.

By the nature of a War Diary this has to cover events in a very general manner and it therefore reflects an overview of what happened, omitting much specific detail. An obvious expedient really, as each participant in an event will experience different aspects and see the picture in a slightly different light. Not surprisingly, John's record is eminently more detailed. His account is almost 'novel like' in structure and clearly shows both the confusion of battle and the emotional strain this puts on the individual.

In particular, the events during the second night of battle show that there is more to combat than simply charging or shooting at the enemy;

> "..... [we] had been engaged in a series of advances, attacks and counter attacks all day [11th September]. It was now well into the night ..... and [we were] leading the advance through a chilly, dark, clear night along a firm and fairly wide dirt road which wended its way through woods, fields and occasional farm yards.

> There was little or no moon and the midnight blue sky overhead contained but a few wisps of cloud. The dark ..... earth of the ploughed fields and pasture land made it difficult to distinguish its occupants or any movement ..... even with the aid of night glasses which each Commander carried slung from his neck. It was said that the Germans intended to make a stand "on the Albert Canal" and Four Troop was approaching the outskirts of Gheel, so progress was at a steady, cautious pace with anxious Commanders, their heads poking out of their 'butterfly' lids of the turrets, peering through night glasses keenly and warily, every nerve so strained that it became difficult to distinguish between real and imagined movement.

> I ..... was third tank in line. From all around us came the sound of battle. It was as though we were in the centre of a huge ring of massed big drums which had been orchestrated to accompany the sporadic rattle of machine guns, punctuated with the 'blap', 'blap', 'blap' of mortars exploding round us, the higher pitched 'splat' of the single-shot rifles and the constant whine of shells passing over ..... . The flashes from the guns ..... also supplied a ..... large flickering circle of illumination which silhouetted trees, hedgerows, buildings and ..... the procession of tanks with straining Commanders staring with intense concentration ..... .

> In order to use my senses to their fullest capacity, I had one ear piece of my headset on my ear, whilst the other was adjusted simply to keep the first in place and so leave one ear free to take in the noises around me. I deemed

one ear sufficient for the radio and endeavoured to put the other to use in supplementing my eyesight, in the event that if anything outside moved and I failed to see it, hopefully, I might just hear it.

There was not a great deal to be heard on the radio at the present time for, as a matter of battle routine, radio silence was, as far as humanly possible, observed and, since all the crew was tense and concentrating on the eyepieces of periscopes, there was little or no conversation between us. After all, we were going into the lion's den, had not each man his job to do well ..... undivided attention to the main purpose was paramount.

I glanced behind me from time to time to ensure that Four Charlie, the last tank in the Troop, was following me and at roughly the right interval. It always was.

However well (or badly) we saw, somebody at least saw better for suddenly and completely without warning shells began to hit the ground and burst all round us. They seemed to be coming from our front left, from a spot concealed from our direct view by a group of buildings, probably a farm ..... . An urgent command from our Troop leader brought us all round to his right in a sweeping curve ..... and we came into line spread over some hundred [yards or so]. At least such was the intention, ... the ground was too soft and there was no means of knowing what else was crawling over it.

The first part of the manoeuvre worked admirably, apart from the fact that the enemy gunners followed our movement ..... or they were lucky in ..... probing for us. I had taken my swing to maintain distance between myself and Four Able ..... as I came up on its right. Four Charlie, however, came up and crossed behind me to move level ..... on my left when he should have been on my right. I knew there was nothing much I could do about it except perhaps to move further out to the right and allow him to come up between me and Four Able. I swung out further ..... and then it happened.

The right track hit a patch of very soft soil and sank, bringing us to halt. Ritchie [Driver], without being told, tried reverse. She wouldn't move ..... "Hold it, Ritchie" ..... drill type commands were never my strong point, I was only a part-time soldier. " ..... go easy or we'll dig in ..... forward very gently ..... stop ..... left stick ..... forward." He did so and she seemed to be spinning slowly round the left track, then she shuddered, gave a sigh and slipped back to rest her belly on the earth. "Right stop..... ", I said, " ..... we'll have to get a tow." There was a brief flurry of suggestions from the crew, each dying away as the futility of each one was realised. "Is our tow rope O.K. .....?" I asked. " ..... of course ..... ." I tried to get Four Charlie on the air, intending to ask him to come over and help us but to no avail. I was silent and inactive for a moment during which I again became aware of the sounds of battle ..... "God" I thought, "I'm going to have to go out in that and find Four Charlie." I didn't want to go, but what else could I do? ..... .

"Listen, lads" I said on the inter-com, "I'm going to see if I can find Four Charlie to give us a tow. I'll get the hawser off and lay it out first and, if he's got one we'll lay his out too and join them together. That will keep him off the soft ground. Keep the gun pointed towards the enemy and keep a good look- out. Don't forget I am out there and before you shoot anybody make bloody sure it's not me ..... Gassy, look out on top while I am outside ..... . Use the gun if you have to - and if you can." ..... . I disconnected my headset and looked around me. I couldn't see a thing. Was the enemy infantry round us? Where the hell was Four Charlie? I peered into the darkness and waited for the flash of the firing guns and the explosions of shells to illuminate the field but still I saw nothing. ..... I hoisted myself out of the turret and slid down to the ground. I stayed close to the side of the tank to look round again, but the gun flashes revealed no more than I had already seen.

The first bit was easy. I faced the tank and unshackled the end of the hawser which was secured on the top of the sponson, the other end being already shackled to the lugs on the front of the tank. I pulled it and dragged it out to its full extent ahead of the tank, returned to where I had dropped from the turret and peered out into the darkness.

"I wonder if the field is mined" I thought "..... Where did I last see Four Charlie? ..... With a bit of luck I might stumble into his tracks ..... ."

I had stood there long enough. I set off in the soft, clinging soil. 'Burph', 'Burph', 'Burph'. Three shells burst on the ground in rapid succession. I flung myself down ..... lay a moment and then shook myself. "Get up and get going, they have to reload. Now's the time to move." I jumped up, ran and stumbled, almost blindly on for about a minute, then slowed. ..... I was walking slowly ..... then again they came. I was so absorbed in thought I hardly got down, hardly lower in fact than a kneeling position, and I heard no shrapnel whistling through the air. ..... my confidence was growing. ..... [then I saw] a dark shape ..... A tank? Yes. I had a three-quarter side view of her, a Sherman without doubt. ..... I raised my arms and shouted. Futile, of course. I dropped my arms and plodded briskly on. I was so excited I forgot the timing [for incoming salvos of shells]. 'Burph', 'Burph', 'Burph'. The tank was illuminated, but so was I. There was no mistaking the briefly visible head and shoulders between the butterfly lids of the turret. Sergeant Carr, helmet square on head, headphones square on ears, microphone in hand, slightly crouched; busy with the business of war.

"Sergeant" I shouted, "Sergeant." Amidst all that noise it was unlikely he heard me but he must have sensed a presence for he turned towards me before the light of the last flash had wholly died away. I heard him. "Oh my God. A Gerry," he said, "Traverse right." I held up my arms in the gesture of surrender and waved them. "No. No No. Don't shoot, Sergeant, it's me, Corporal Cropper." and I began to run towards him, arms aloft. More explosions rent the air and I saw the black gaping mouth of the seventy-five sweep round and down ..... . If only I can get under that gun ..... and up against the tank before it is fired, I'll stand a chance. ..... with a final desperate burst of effort I realised it was now pointing over my right shoulder and would not depress further. I reached the side of the tank and, spread-eagled, I pressed myself as tightly against it as I could, eyes closed, gulping huge mouthfuls of air, waiting for the explosion that mercifully never came.

Sergeant Carr leaned over the turret and with one ear piece lifted from an ear listened whilst between gasps for breath I explained our predicament. We now had to make a similar trek back to Four Baker, but this time it didn't seem quite so bad. I had company and, although I walked in front of the tank, six sets of eyes were keeping a look-out and my back was guarded. In the darkness I lined Four Charlie up, unshackled its hawser, connected it to the one I had laid out from Four Baker and, thanks to the fact that we had not struggled too hard to extract Four Baker unaided, she was soon back on reasonably solid ground. ..... I climbed back in ..... It was like going back to a home fireside after being out in a wild raging storm.

I gave them the bare bones of my story. "Well, you know Sergeant Carr's deaf, don't you?" said Keith [Cornish]. ..... " ..... What's he doing in a tank then?" [I asked] "Oh, I don't think he was always deaf. Probably stood near a gun when it went off. There's a war on, and he just carried on." I began to wonder, was that why he had come up on my left instead of my right - hadn't he heard the instruction and from our actions just assumed we had to scatter. Another thing. When I found him he wasn't a great distance from where I'd last seen him and that must have been well over an hour ago. ..... . "Forward, Ritchie. Right stick." We moved on, checking our progress by gun flashes, and eventually arrived in line with Baker Four and Four Able which were standing fifty yards or more apart, noses up to a thick shrubby hedgerow. ..... once again I could see no sign of Four Charlie.

..... after a time it became apparent ..... that gunfire from somewhere was zoning in on [us]. I therefore backed out and came up into position again about ten yards further to the right, from where we continued our bombardment. I had by now quite forgotten Four Charlie but only realised it when I heard the sound of tank tracks coming from my rear left. I swung round and peered into the darkness with my night glasses for some seconds before I was able to pick out the dark shape. A Sherman? Yes, a Sherman, unmistakably a Sherman. It must be Four Charlie. He must have spotted me for he veered left and came up towards the line between myself and Four Able. I watched him as he approached the hedgerow. .....

He paused at the hedge. Taking up position, I thought. Now we are complete, but no. After a momentary hesitation, he began to advance again. He crashed through the hedgerow and began slowly to advance. The troop leader broke radio silence. "Baker Four, which of my babies is advancing? Baker Four. Over." There was no answer. On the inter-com, to no-one in particular, I said, "It's Four Charlie. He's not answering. Keith said he was deaf. But his operator's not deaf, or is he?" "Harry [Thomas]? Oh, well," said Keith, "Old Harry's never on net." "Baker Four to babies. Report signals. Baker Four, over." Radio silence had been broken again. "Four Able, strength five. Over." "Four Baker, strength five. Over." A brief silence, then, "Roger. Four Charlie, signals. Over" Still Four Charlie did not respond. Again, I spoke to my crew, "He's not answering." "I'll bet old Harry's not on net", said Keith. I was watching and Four Charlie suddenly did a left turn and moved along our line to the left. "Oh. I think he's heard." I said, "He's turned left. Probably going to swing round the other end of the line." ..... Four Charlie was now out of my range of vision. It was now ..... less than two hours from dawn ..... we were all very tired and settled down to a watching and waiting sort of operation, each dozing a little in turn.

..... when I awakened, dawn was breaking. ..... The hedgerow was nothing as thick as ..... I had imagined it to be, but there was a ground mist and we weren't in much danger of being seen at that stage. I felt we might have to move to better cover a little later on. ..... The mist lifted very slowly as daylight took over from night and eventually I was able to pick out Four Able. I waved to Robbo, whose head just appeared above the turret and he waved back. Eventually I was able to see Baker Four but there was no sign of life there. There was still no sign of Four Charlie. .....

As visibility increased I began to get a little anxious. I did not know where the enemy was and so far I could not see the place we had fired on in the night. Also I had no means of knowing whether, when the mist lifted completely, we would be visible to its occupants or not. I still couldn't see Four Charlie and there was still no sign of life from Baker Four. Minutes later the radio came to life. It was the usual netting drill routine and, again,

Four Charlie did not answer. .....

[Whilst discussing where Four Charlie could be] we were interrupted by a call from Baker Four instructing "All babies' leaders to me, on foot in five." ..... I grabbed my map case and jumped down, straightened my tank suit ..... and walked along the hedgerow towards Baker Four. .....

"First of all," said the Troop leader, "I've some bad news for you. Four Charlie was knocked out last night." ..... "The crew are all either dead or have been taken prisoner. The Germans are believed to have been seen lifting one of them on to a stretcher, so one, at least may be a prisoner even though he is injured."

..... "We don't know how badly but he is a stretcher case. He was knocked out on the other side of that barn" pointing to a building about fifty yards away. "I called him repeatedly to get into line but I got no answer. His 'A' set must have gone for a burton."

..... " ..... Now. This is how we start today. We're down to three in the troop. When we'll get a replacement I don't know. Intelligence tells us that the main German force has withdrawn about five miles along this road but he's left a rearguard in Gheel. It's our job to drive them out. The Squadron will move at seven. We will join them here" (he indicated positions on his map) "and First Troop will lead. We bring up the rear. You and I, Robbo, will be ready to move at quarter to, then we'll move off to the rendezvous. Now, you John. What's your position like down there?"

"Not too good. A bit exposed, I think. I was firing on a position last night and if it is still occupied they may be able to see me when the mist clears. They had me pinpointed pretty well last night."

"Oh. Well, when I move out, move up here and take up my position. I don't think the mist will have fully cleared by then. They are bringing in the dead from last night's affair and they will be laid out in one of the fields on the right of the approach road we came along last night. I want you to go along and see if you can find any of our lads amongst them. If you can, remove their personal possessions from the bodies and one of the identity discs they should have round their necks. Make each set into a separate little bundle and you can hand them to me when you rejoin us about, say 0900 hours, here." His finger again pointed out a position on the map. "O.K?"

"Yes Sir."

"Have either of you any questions?"

In unison, we both said "No Sir."

"Right then. Time for a brew."

Robbo and I walked back towards out tanks, silently. Each occupied with his own thoughts. Half way back to Four Able, Robbo lifted his head. "Did you know Sergeant Carr was deaf?"

"No, I didn't know," I said. "I believe some people thought he might have been."

"Mm. Perhaps it was just a rumour." ..... "See you later."

I walked on to Four Baker, clambered back into her and looked around. The mist still obscured us from the point at which we had fired last night but it seemed to me to be getting fairly close to the stage at which we would be revealed. I slid my map case into its place and told the crew of the events and our instructions.

"Ye Gods!" was the response and Keith, more to himself than to anyone in particular, said "Old Harry never was on net." We were all silent awhile then "What about a brew?" said Tutin."

A short while later, the crew of Four Baker moved position as instructed and settled to the business of eating and cleaning up the debris of battle from themselves and the vehicle. For John this was a way of delaying what had to be done, but all to soon duty called;

"I didn't march and I didn't rush. I was Shakespeare's schoolboy, 'creeping like a snail unwillingly to school.' I was going somewhere I didn't want to go, to do something I didn't want to do, but it was something I had to do. Last night, when alive, they had done something for me. Today, whilst I was alive, I must do something for them, or their families. I walked on. In the field, at first, I saw nothing. I walked slowly forward, then I saw them, a line of soldiers in uniform, lying dead, feet towards me. I approached them. Better start at one end of the line and walk along it to the other. Slowly I walked along the line searching. Sometimes I had to step between them to get a better look at a face, half turned away, or a regimental insignia that was partly obscured. They lay in various postures and conditions though, curiously, none of them appeared to be grossly mutilated. Somewhere, I wondered, on the other side of the line, was there possibly a German soldier doing just what I was doing and even, perhaps, thinking what I was thinking? Count your dead.

The men lay in the order in which they had been brought in from the battlefield. No separate messes here. Officer rubbed shoulders with private, sergeant major with corporal, ... All had the same waxen pallor, some eyes were closed, some open, but all unseeing. .....

..... At last. I had found one of the lads. Old Harry, who was never on net. He lay as I had seen him in life when asleep. I touched him. He was icy cold, and somewhat rigid. Carefully I removed one of his identity discs. I did it as if he were asleep and I didn't want to waken him. Then I turned to the reprehensible task of going through his pockets. I tied the pitifully few worthless little items together with his identity disc in his handkerchief. I stood before him a few seconds as a sort of homage. I didn't pray. I didn't think. It wasn't homage really, just a sort of 'Cheerio Harry'. I did it once more with another member of the crew[1]. [The others must have been] carried away ..... by the [Gerries]."

It was now early on the morning of the 12th September and it was not until the 13th that Gheel was finally cleared of the German rearguard. The price, as we have already seen, was very high though and it was generally reported that had the SRY Squadrons engaged (B and C) not been so aggressive in their actions then the bridgehead would undoubtedly have been lost. They now desperately needed time to compose themselves, but were to have just 4 days to recover, repair and replenish before the commencement of operation Market Garden and the push to secure the bridges at Eindhoven, Grave, Nijmegen and Arnhem.

For 4 Troop this not only meant a replacement crew and vehicle for the unfortunate Four Charlie, but 'Pin-Up Girl' had been showing signs of wear from the high mileage over the previous weeks and was sent for refurbishment. Her replacement, another 75mm Sherman Mk III, number T232668, was quickly turned into a home from home though and as this was a 'Sherwood Rangers' vehicle it was felt appropriate to give the new chariot a new name.

"B" Squadron, paused on a road in Germany. From right to left are: Georgie Wright, Ted King, Gordon, Pinker, Frank Milner and Jack Snedker.
The man on the extreme left is unknown, as is the dog !

> "It was Fred Gasson that named her, he was keen on that sort of thing and came up with Blue Light Special. He produced a pot of white paint liberated from some store or other, just enough to paint the name on."

A 'Blue Light'[2] was military slang for a rumour during WWII, a fact my father swears to and who am I to doubt his word. Strangely though, a blue light signified something very different in the Great War - an Officers brothel. Isn't it strange how the use of language changes over time!

NOTES:

[1] It appears that Four Charlie moved forward to engage an 88mm anti-tank gun, which she was later credited with destroying. Sergeant Carr had been carried away badly wounded and was to survive the war as a German POW, following treatment for his wounds. The two crewmen killed and identified by John were both ex XXIVth Lancers, Troopers Harry Thomas and Henry Randle. The other two crew, also ex XXIVth men - Troopers L C Heavens and A Rose, ended up in Stalag 344 as P.O.W.s. Should any relatives of those killed ever read this, John's account goes on to remark on his surprise that neither men had been disfigured.

[2] Despite much searching I have been unable to establish the origin of the phrase 'a blue light' in connection with a rumour, although I have come across numerous other references to it in this context.

CHAPTER 7- CASUALTIES OF WAR

As anyone who has served with the military will tell you, all the equipment and kit you are issued with remains the property of H M Forces, so if you lose anything then you must pay for it. To keep things above board and official, therefore, you sign for it. Then there can never be any argument that you were the last possessor of whatever offending item has 'gone west' and you can be charged accordingly.

It will come as no surprise, therefore, that on accepting delivery of T232668, Corporal Cropper was obliged to sign a receipt, upon the completion of which he was presented with a copy of the document and a 'new' tank.

This receipt is still with his memoirs and attests to the vehicle being fully tested and ready for use, however;

> "We always T & A'd[1] our own gun. We'd use hairs to make a cross over the muzzle end of the gun, stuck down with a little grease, and then took the firing pin out so that we could look down the breech. If we could get cotton that was better because it was more visible, but a couple of hairs from your head worked just as well.
>
> Of course, you had to make sure you got the cotton or hair off afterwards or firing an H.E. shell with it in the barrel could cause an explosion."

In addition;

> "The Sherman had a .50 calibre browning machine gun mounted on a moveable ring around the cupola, for use against aircraft. It was a bulky thing and more in the way than anything else so I, for one, always took it off and passed it to the infantry or simply threw it away. In fact I don't recall ever seeing any of our tanks with one on - I think everyone did the same.
>
> It was a bad idea anyway - if we had to bail out the damn thing would have been in the way and it could have turned a minimal chance of escape into a virtually impossible one.
>
> Fortunately, what was left of the mounting made a convenient place to hang my small pack!"

A convenience that may just have saved his life a little later on.

D-Day for operation 'Market Garden' was the 17th September and the SRY were on notice to move, once Grave had fallen. The weather was fine that day and the American troops progressed well, taking Veghel bridge. The next day saw Grave bridge taken and the tanks were moved forward to the Escault canal. By nightfall they had begun to advance again but the weather was worsening and news arrived of the problems at Arnhem. On the 19th they pressed on further, but the weather was still bad. Due to the constant state of alert, foul weather and continual stopping and starting the crews, not unusually, had to spend all their time in their metal homes.

This unrelenting pressure began to make its mark;

> "The progress was relentless and we were all dog tired, driving day and night with the steady rocking of the tank. We were so tired in fact that at one point Ritchie, who was driving, fell asleep at the sticks and as the rest of the crew were out cold I had to climb out of the turret, down the front of the tank and grab him by the shoulders to shake him awake. Fortunately his hatch was open so I could get at him fairly easily.
>
> And all the time the tank just kept going forward - it never stopped moving."

One of the drills not taught at Bovington but acquired very quickly on landing in France, was to do with one of the most basic needs of the human race - the need to go to the toilet. Unlike modern trains and luxury coaches, the Sherman tank did not have an on board 'loo' so the crew were left with three basic options. They could wait until it was convenient to go outside, go outside whenever the need took them or simply 'go' in the tank whenever necessary. Clearly the first two options were not very practical, so in order to relieve themselves whilst in the tank;

> "We used empty shell cases to pee in, and for whatever else was required. Peeing wasn't too much of a problem, but if it was the other you had to be very careful because if the tank rocked or hit a bump you were in serious danger of giving yourself an unwanted re- bore!"

And once relieved;

"We simply tossed the shell cases out of the turret."

Due to the volume of men and material pushing forward and the strength of the opposition, the roads were congested and progress was slow. By the evening of the 20th after 72 hard and tiring miles, they finally met up with the American 82nd Airborne division at Grave itself. Here they halted their advance and were to provide armoured support for the Americans on the high ground around Dekkensward and Grosbeek. At this time, the allied line ran from Nijmegen through Urbergen, Beek, Grafwogen and Enbrook.

On the following day, the 21st September, "B" Squadron moved into the Nijmegen sector and their Recce Troop crossed the border into Germany to have a look around. The first British troops to enter Germany, all sixteen of them[2].

For the rest of the Squadron the next few days were spent helping the American troops to straighten out their line in the Mook sector, providing mobile artillery support and firmly establishing themselves as the first British troops to enter Germany with more trips across the border;

> "The Americans were a very appreciative lot and were very informal as far as rank etc was concerned, which suited me down to the ground as we were not exactly the most 'formal' of military units either."

Indeed, they could be quite generous too on occasion;

> "Whilst in the Nijmegen sector a Yank came along one day, climbed up on the tank and gave me a brand new American tank-suit. It was really warm and well cut, much better than ours, when you could get them. Most people just wore their battledress and I can't claim to be a lover of tanksuits, they were a bit restrictive. But when you were constantly in action, particularly if the weather was cold, they were a boon.."

On the 2nd October, the tanks supported the American 325th Combat team in a set piece engagement and John became a 'Cropper' in every sense of the word.

A common misconception about tanks is that they can cross just about any type of terrain with ease, due to their caterpillar tracks. The truth, though, is not so dramatic. Certainly the tracks do make it easier for tanks to go where wheeled vehicles have difficulty, but they cannot simply travel with impunity. Tracked vehicles are particularly vulnerable if their underside, the bottom of the vehicle between the two tracks, comes into contact with the ground. If this happens then the turning of the tracks simply whips out the ground from below them, settling the tank firmly on the ground. As a consequence recovery can then become a major task, so crews would usually call for help sooner rather than later if they started to bog down;

> "Provided the tank did not go down to its belly you could usually free it fairly easily, either alone or with a bit of help. At one stage we had been pressing forward under fire and my right track slipped over a bank. It quickly became obvious that we couldn't get out alone so I radio'd for the recovery vehicle[3] to come and give me a pull. Well at first they didn't want to come near because we were under fire and when they did reach me I was the one who had to jump down and attach the hawser.
>
> They rushed the job though and instead of pulling me out they skewed me over until the belly grounded - and then took off and left me. Then an officer came up, I don't know where from, and started to give me hell over the position we were in. My reply was far from military and unprintable - he just turned and went away!"

A few days later they were relieved by the Coldstream Guards, but when they were to return just over 72 hours later;

> "As I pulled into position an American soldier walked up to the front of the tank and brushed away the camouflage covering our markings. When he saw the 'Fox's Mask'[4] he looked up and said "Thank god you guys are back, I know your Guards are supposed to be the cream but if we ever needed any fire support they had to get permission from the Brigadier before they fired a shot"."

For the 'informal' men of the SRY;

> "If we were asked by the infantry to shell a position, we did and worried about getting permission later."

For this particular 'Yeomanry' Corporal, there were similar feelings about the 'regimental' bull of the Guards;

"We were once moving forward, on the march into Holland, and as the country opened up the Guards Armoured, who were leading, deployed either side of the road so that they would be advancing in line instead of column. I don't know why. The thing was that the roads in that area were built up with a fairly firm base. The fields, on the other hand, were very soft going and totally unsuitable for armour.

Needless to say, their tanks very quickly bogged down and the advance came to a dead halt. At least theirs did, we sailed past them on the road and took the lead."

On another occasion;

"We were to cross a bridge that had been badly damaged, but was just about passable for tanks. [It was] under fire of course. Well the Guards put their tanks two abreast and set out across. It was unbelievable as there was a big hole in this thing leaving just about enough room for one tank to pass.

It came as no surprise to me that one of the two leading tanks went straight down the hole."

When finally relieved on the 15th, John was in for a treat - leave in Brussels;

"All men on leave were billeted in an army hostel, with a bed and small cabinet for your gear. On this occasion Keith and I went sightseeing on the first afternoon because neither of us were great boozers or into some of the more wild things that the men got up to when on leave.

For me, a naive and fairly unsophisticated lad from the country, the sights were absorbing and we wandered around drinking them in. Going down one street we came across a shop window with women sitting inside, some knitting others sewing, chatting or reading papers. They were prostitutes and the pair of us stood, like children with no money outside a toy shop window at Christmas - looking at the sights in wonderment!"

By the early evening the city became quieter as the locals retired for their evening meals but the two men, away from the war for the first time in months, continued to enjoy the freedom of being able to wander around at will;

"Keith and I were looking through another shop window when a voice piped up from behind and a bloke said "You are not enjoying Brussels very much at this moment I think", referring to it being quiet by now. We both turned round and politely told him that of course we were. However, he invited us to his home for a meal and was very insistent.

It turned out that he was either the Lord Chief Justice or a senior appeal court judge, a grey haired old man with a somewhat younger wife in her 40's. They insisted that we stay with them and were given a massive bedroom with a huge double bed. The rest of our leave was spent in luxury."

The Squadron was still at rest on his return so it was back to the never ending tasks of maintenance and replenishment, punctuated by the chance to use the services of a mobile bath unit and a cinema in Nijmegen. As far as the former was concerned it would have been nice to have had a proper bath before going on leave but both John and Keith had already had the luxury of a 'real' bath in their 5 star billet. With regard to the cinema;

"I never went to an army film show in all my time with the forces, I don't know why but I never fancied going."

Madame Heetveld, with John standing behind. Taken shortly after the Judge's death on one of the brief leaves in Brussels

On the 21st it was back to the front line again, this time in support of the other American Airborne division, the 101st 'Screaming Eagles', on an island position in the river Waal opposite Arnhem. Due to the constant fighting there throughout the month this area had already disintegrated into a dark, battle scarred shambles. This situation was not to improve either, as in ten days' hard fighting alone, between the 18th and 28th September, the Brigade lost 7 Officers and 83 other ranks in simply holding this position.

Eventually relieved on the 2nd November, it was back to billets at Winssen for more maintenance and yet more leave, John managed another day and a half in Brussels;

> "[And] back to the Heetveld's and the lap of luxury. In fact, every visit to Brussels later on was spent with them even though the Judge died shortly after that second visit."

Upon his return from leave he learned that the SRY had a new task, to support the 84th US division who were currently engaged at Asch. This time, however, the tanks were not expected to move under their own steam and transporters arrived to take them on the long march south. Once there, and following the unloading of their tanks, they moved on to Paulenberg, a small German mining town which had been reduced to rubble by the fighting and was now used as a rest area by the American forces. The whole place was a sea of mud and the quarters, in old cellars, were not at all appealing;

> "Our billet was sodden, there was a thick piled carpet on the floor but it was like walking in squelchy mud. We ended up sleeping in the tank because it was so damp and wet."

Drills and exercises are a common feature of military life even for troops in a war zone and just as in peace time, concentration by the ordinary soldier to the detail is fleeting at best. The Army overcomes this lackadaisical attitude by the simple expedient of constant repetition. Do the same exercises again and again and eventually the participants act like automatons, when the appropriate situation occurs they simply follow the appropriate drill without thinking - at least that is what was intended.

4 Troop undertook their share of drilling in common with most other armoured units. Usually on the days when they had been pulled back from the front

line, but not always with conviction as we have already seen. The process of constant repetition did work though.

During the advance towards the next objective, Geilenkirchen, the Troop Commander had temporarily left the confines of Baker 4 and was sitting on the front of a Bren Carrier, which was leading the ungainly column of Shermans along a country road through open fields. Every now and then a distant farm building or isolated haystack hove into view. Apart from that there was little to punctuate the scenery, yet the column advanced slowly as they were pushing forward through occupied territory and isolated pockets of Germans had been reported in the area.

It was about four o'clock in the afternoon and yet another haystack came up on the left flank. This time, unknown to the column, the haystack covered a slit trench in which a small party of determined soldiers watched the approaching vehicles.

Order of march behind the leading carrier was Baker 4, 4 Able , 4 Baker and 4 Charlie bringing up the rear. Behind him, and at the appropriate distance, the rest of "B" Squadron followed.

As the carrier came within about 50 yards of the haystack a sudden noise announced the discharge of a Panzerfaust. This was quickly followed by a thud as the offending projectile passed across its front plate, taking the Officer's leg with it as it continued on into the field behind. Within seconds, and just as if part of a formation dancing team performance, every turret of 4 Troop traversed towards the haystack.

This, almost effortless, manoeuvre was then followed by what sounded like a single report as all four guns fired in unison and the base of the haystack, together with its hidden protagonists, disappeared from view.

> "I just reacted, we all did - no thought, it was just like being on a training exercise"

The Troop Leader was passed back for treatment and within minutes the column, and the war, moved on.

By now the allies were drawn up against the Siegfried line, with the British

XXX Corps holding the right flank of the British forces and the US 9th Army holding the left flank of the American advance. At this very point there was a salient in the German defences, where the Siegfried line bent around the town of Geilenkirchen. In view of the experience of XXX Corps commander, Lieutenant- General Horrocks, command of both the American and British forces was placed in his hands and he was given orders to straighten out the allied line. A task recognised as being fraught with difficulties, no less because of the long term German propaganda extolling the might of the Westwall defences.

The U.S. 84th Division comprised of the 333rd, 334th and 335th Infantry Regiments, who were better known as the 'Railsplitters' after their divisional sign which featured a red axe splitting a white log. They were fresh troops, not long in Europe, and this was to be their first action. The arrival of the Sherwood Rangers as supporting armour for their assault, therefore, was welcomed by the Americans and did much to increase confidence in these 'green' troops - a fact recorded in a number of GI's diaries at the time.

To the south of Geilenkirchen itself was a railway embankment which formed a very effective tank obstacle. In addition, the whole area was supplemented by minefields and interconnected pillboxes, which were to become an all too familiar feature as the troops pressed on into the Siegfried line itself. Indeed, this point in the line was probably the strongest section of the 'Westwall' defences. For the initial advance though, the 2nd US Armoured division had been allocated the clearance of this particular feature but the men of the SRY were soon to get their own share.

On the 16th the American assault began and on the 17th "B" Squadron moved into their start positions.

One of the Regiment's ARVs. Note that the turret has been removed.

Their attack commenced before dawn on the 18th with the aid of 'artificial moonlight'[5], supplied by 1127 Searchlight Battery. Flail tanks moved first to clear a path through the minefield, followed by Churchill tanks who laid fascines over the railway tracks to make crossing the embankment easier for the armour. Next came the men of the SRY who set to work on the pillboxes. Initially the going was difficult because of the mud, coupled with difficulties in getting the tanks across the railway line, but progress was steady and by noon the first objective had been reached with no casualties.[6] The Sherwood Rangers had become the first British Regiment to attack into the Siegfried Line. There was not much time to dwell on this though as they pressed on towards Geilenkirchen with the day drawing on;

> "We were pushing across open ground and suspected that it may be mined, so movement was slow. To add to that we were under constant small arms fire and then they put a 'stonk' down on us. A few moments after it began one landed immediately behind me and I wasn't quite quick enough in taking cover, my head and right hand were still above the turret as the shrapnel struck."

Fortunately John, as usual, had hung his small pack over the back of the turret. This took some pieces of shrapnel and protected his shoulders and neck. His helmet saved his head and his neck received nothing more than a severe bruising. Unfortunately, his right hand was not so lucky. Wounded, bruised and bleeding John was forced to go back for treatment;

> "After handing over the tank to Keith I jumped down, taking my small pack and revolver with me. As there was a possibility of mines I walked in the tanks tracks back towards the rear - I could walk fine, with just a bruised neck and my right hand bandaged and bleeding. Strangely though, although there was lead flying around everywhere, no one seemed to be shooting at me.
>
> I had only got about 100 yards from the tank when I met two American stretcher bearers coming towards me. They said something like "Jump on here buddy" but I told them I was fine and could cope on my own. Clearly they had no intention of going any further forward and literally pushed me down on the stretcher."

He was carried, somewhat reluctantly, back to the forward aid post and then to a casualty clearing station. From there he was moved to Ward C4 Louvain hospital, which was a fully equipped facility situated in a Convent and staffed by Nuns from a nursing order, together with some Q.A.R.A.N.C. nurses and an R.A.M.C. medical team.[7]

> "I had been there a few days and all that happened was a nurse came round once a day and removed the bandage, then the Surgeon came and had a look and then the nurse came back and re-dressed the wound. The process took about half an hour and during that time I would pick the little bits of metal out of my hand.
>
> My wound wasn't severe but I could still write, with considerable difficulty, and my fingers were beginning to get very stiff. Somewhat concerned I decided to speak with the Surgeon on his next round. His response shocked me a little as he said he wasn't impressed with the wound, going on to ask my army occupation and finishing with "..... you don't need to write do you?". I responded in kind.
>
> "It's not your business to be impressed," I said, "It's your job to heal." Which was quite a risk when you think about it as he was a Major and I was only a Corporal, but I was quite annoyed at the time. He just turned to the nurse though and told her to put me down for an x-ray."

The next day John was operated on and two pieces of shrapnel, which had been against the tendons in his hand, were removed. Both about the size of a polo mint. Dexterity returned soon after.

Two very small pieces remained and he carries them still, although over the passage of time one has worked its way to the knuckle of his middle finger and the other has lodged at the base of his thumb. Both easily felt through the skin.

Whilst in hospital he had lost all contact with his Regiment and had no news from his crew probably, he thought, due to them still being in action. Imagine his surprise, therefore, when he was walking round a few days after the operation and saw Ritchie, swathed in bandages and sitting up in bed.

It transpired that Keith had received a field promotion to Lance Corporal on the day John was wounded and the tank struggled on with one crewman short. The following day Lt. Charles took command as his own tank had been brewed-up, but shortly after they too were hit by an 88mm round and Ritchie got burnt when getting out. As far as he knew, all the others were killed.[8]

Shocked, John eventually returned to his own bed and he was not to see Ritchie again after he left hospital as fate had something else in store. News arrived that his mother was very ill and he was granted compassionate leave. On the 28th December, therefore, he travelled to Eigenbilzen where he eventually boarded Dakota, no. KG372, for a flight to Northolt in England.

Marching the easy way!
One of the Troop's Sherman tanks on the back of a transporter

NOTES:

1 Test and Adjust

2 Commanded by Lieutenant Ian McKay.

3 For ARV's (Armoured Recovery Vehicles) the Sherwood Rangers used Sherman tanks with their turrets removed.

4 Badge of the 8th Armoured Brigade

5 A technique whereby strong searchlights were shone on low cloud, giving a dim reflection on the surface of the ground sufficient for men to work by without exposing them too much to enemy observers.

6 No human casualties. Three tanks were completely destroyed by mines and a fourth was damaged but later recovered.

7 QARANC - Queen Alexandra's Royal Army Nursing Corps. RAMC - Royal Army Medical Corps.

8 In fact 'Toots' Tutin had only been wounded. Lt Charles, Keith Cornish and Fred Gasson had not been so lucky though, all three died in the tank. One of the things Ritchie said to John whilst in Hospital was that the others would not have died if he had still been with them, but no further details of this conversation have survived. During the research for this book I uncovered an account of the demise of one of the SRY tanks at Geilenkirchen. It appears that this tank pulled up to some American troops, who were under fire, and began to engage their assailants. Within a short time it was targeted and hit by an 88mm round. This removed one of the tracks but instead of baling out before the next round came, as the American observers expected, the crew stayed with their tank and continued firing. They got off three more rounds before the next 88mm shell ploughed straight into them, finishing the tank off. Only two of the crew got out of the front hatches and these may well have been Toots and Ritchie. Undoubtedly, a more experienced tank Commander would have realised that a second round would have followed and ordered the crew to bail out, knowing that they had been targeted and were unable to manoeuvre.

CHAPTER 8 - A RELUCTANT COMMAND

The plane taking John back to England carried a large red cross on the side, but perhaps as a reflection of the particularly hard winter, the festive season and limited operations, it was filled with seemingly fit men;

> "Shortly after I boarded and sat myself down a WAAF Nurse came along. As the plane was fairly packed with men I offered her my seat but she told me that she was actually part of the crew. It transpired that they usually carried wounded but that particular flight didn't carry any. Despite that she was supposed to stand up throughout the flight in case of need.
>
> This was not the brush off I first thought as after we were in the air she came back and we spent the whole flight chatting. Strangely, I never asked her name."

A sign of the times no doubt for many, both military and civilian, chance acquaintances were very common and all too brief. Consequently, names ceased to have as much importance as they do today.

John's leave pass was valid to the 16th January so in the time available he managed to squeeze in a little more than planned, he married the WREN who visited him a few days before the Invasion. His mother was not at all well though and her poor state encouraged him to seek a leave extension;

> "I duly turned up at the office in Liverpool and was marched in to a room where an Officer was seated, lying back in his chair with his feet up on the desk. There was I, stood at attention, and he casually lolled back in his chair and asked my business.
>
> After hearing my explanation I was dismissed with no sufficient grounds and my return date remained unchanged."

The experience had not impressed the young soldier, so he took an extension anyway - an extra four days. On reporting back to a transit camp he was not surprised to be placed under arrest.

> "It was strange really, I was under arrest but you wouldn't have thought so. Things were no different for me than they were for anyone else, although

that was probably because I didn't appreciate quite what I was or was not allowed to do.

For instance, I learned later that I was not allowed in the NAFFI. Of course I was in and out of the place all the time I was there."

His reception upon arriving back at his Regiment though was a bit of a surprise;

"I was taken to the R.S.M. who marched me in to the C.O., Lt Col Christopherson, to answer the charge. On hearing my answer the Colonel simply dismissed the charge and I was marched out again. Once outside the attitude of the R.S.M. changed from a 'Regimental' one to something entirely different. He told me off, not for being A.W.O.L. or for going through the proper channels, but for not taking my problem directly to him. He said that if I ever got in that situation again I was to contact the Regiment and they would sort everything out. You see, the Regiment was like a big family - they looked after their own."

During his absence the regiment had been alternating between periods of action and rest, and the weather had turned bitter with temperatures as much as 35° below. Casualties had not been too heavy but, even so, John was surprised to find himself posted back to his old position in command of 4 Baker. However, this time it was to be different.

Awaiting his arrival was a new tank and a new crew. Instead of the familiarity of the 75mm gun which he had grown to trust, this tank featured the long 17pdr and was a much heavier vehicle altogether. In addition, it sported a petrol engine instead of the more familiar diesel[1];

"How well I remember taking command of her and how reluctant I was. I knew nothing of her 17pdr and I had an aversion to the sluggishness of a 17pdr tank. However, I soon found that I had a crew who could overcome these difficulties very easily."

The crew of a Sherman Firefly was only 4, due to the extra space required for storage of the larger ammunition and more space needed for the breech of the gun. Consequently, they had to manage without a Co-Driver but this didn't make them any less effective as a fighting machine and the new Driver,

Frank Milner, quickly solved the tanks sluggishness with a little bit of D.I.Y. - he removed the governor from the engine, pushing the maximum speed up by an extra 15 miler per hour.

His Gunner, Jack Snedker had no problems with his role either and John recorded, just two days later;

> "I very quickly developed an affection for a gun that could hit and destroy with one shot."

The final place in the crew, the Operator, was taken by Ted King.

In the process of "squeezing in a little more than planned".
13 January 1945

One more change on his return was the new Troop Commander, Lt Hyde, replacing the unfortunate Mr Charles who had been killed at Geilenkirchen. This was not such a traumatic transition though as John took an almost instant liking to the man;

> "He was the kind of chap you got along with, a better Troop Commander we couldn't have wished for."

With the same call-sign it only seemed right that this new tank was also christened 'Blue Light Special', although this time there was a shortage of paint and the letters were a little cruder than on her forbear. Somehow though, that didn't seem too important.

Over the next few days there was plenty of opportunity to 'field test' this new command as his Squadron attacked Selsten, Schandorf and then Kirschoven in completing operation 'Black Cock', the advance from Sittard to Heinsberg. From there it was back to Belgium, first Moll and then Nijmegen, for the next stage of the battle, operation 'Veritable' - the attack on the Reichswald.

During that time he also discovered something else about his new command;

> "..... the 17pdr tanks were the first targeted in any engagement. So we painted a white ring around the barrel, about 1" wide, at the length of a 75mm gun. From there to the end of the muzzle we painted a white, wavy line on the underside of the barrel. Amazingly, if you stood a short distance away it looked just like a 75mm gun. From a long way off, if you had the troop together you had to look very closely to see that one of the tanks was a 17pdr. Only the longer box on the back of the turret really gave us away and by the time Gerry realised that we were there the paint job had bought us those few, precious moments."

On the 7th February the Squadron commenced a softening up barrage on the new objective, with the tanks drawn up in line and engaging in an indirect fire 'sweep'. It was a standard procedure and one carried out often before;

> "It was during this operation that one of the most frightening things for a crew happened, we had a misfire. The fear was that if we had to open the breech then the shell may explode, which meant the end of us. There was a standard drill to go through and it basically involved re-cocking the firing

mechanism and trying to fire again. You were supposed to go through it twice before opening the breech - we did it three times but still no joy, so we had a quick discussion to plan what to do next.

In the end we finally decided that Ted would throw open the breech, I would catch the shell and launch it out of the turret - with absolutely no regard for any infantry that may have been milling around outside of course. So this is what we did and nothing happened.

The next shell didn't fire either, nor the one after that - in the end I jumped out to look at them and found that the firing pin hadn't been striking. I don't know why.

Jack quickly sorted it out by fitting a replacement."

On the 9th, with the barrage completed, each tank loaded a couple of pine logs behind the turret as a counter measure in case of bogging down and to help in crossing slit trenches. Then they took on board some infantry and eventually moved off from Beek, via Krannenburg to Nutterden, on to Thewce and then through the outskirts of Cleve to some high ground west of Louisendorf.

"B" Squadron had taken the lead once more and, as could be expected, drew the first shell-fire from the direction of the Reichswald as they approached Cleve itself. It was understood that the 15th Scottish had actually taken the town so it came as quite a shock when they reached a road block covered by machine gun fire and the ever present Panzerfausts;

"The men riding on the back were most uncomfy - that had been the first and only time we had our troops riding on the back into action and I don't blame them for not being keen, there was lead flying everywhere - and all of it seemingly aimed at us."

The tanks pressed forward but with failing light eventually decided to withdraw for the night. By dawn the next morning the enemy tanks and assault guns could clearly be seen in the distance and a battle soon commenced with two tanks being lost. "A" and "C" Squadrons fared just as badly losing another four between them and, to make things worse, the Germans opened the Rhine dykes and the ground was rapidly flooding - up to two feet in parts. The fighting became scattered and confused but Cleve finally fell on the 11th.

By the 13th the whole of the Reichswald was in British hands and on the 14th, "B" Squadron was back in the lead again. Shelling became intense but luckily casualties were light. On the 16th they were finally pulled back for a short rest and the crew found themselves in billets that were little better than those at Paulenberg, sodden. They chose to sleep in the tank yet again.

Blue Light Special, taken in Goch - March 1945. The crew's billet was in the building on the left of the picture. Note the paintwork on the underside of the barrel.

It seems strange that there was little envy between the infantryman and tankman for their respective roles, as the benefits of riding instead of walking or of not having to be covered in grease and grime whilst carrying out continual vehicle maintenance seem obvious to the casual observer. But the truth was that given the choice, few would trade places.

All were aware of the fate of some of the tank crews and in the fighting since D-Day few had not seen the effects of a 'brewed-up' tank on the crew - burnt skeletons, decapitated bodies and pools of congealing fat that once were men. Even so, the tankmen did not envy their counterparts who were forced to face the enemy fire with little more than a tin hat for protection.

On the 1st March "B" Squadron was detached to support an assault by the East Lanc's on some woods east of the village of Weeze. At mid-day they had assembled before their objective but this time things were a little different;

> "Usually when we worked with infantry they would walk behind. This time they formed four or five rows across our front and we lined up right behind their back rank to provide moving artillery support in place of the 9 mile snipers?"

Ahead of them lay a wide field and on the other side a wood or copse, occupied by enemy infantry with armoured support.

> "When we set off the infantry spread out to about 10 yards between each man. We kept right up to the back line as they charged across the field, firing over their heads on the objective all the time.
>
> I was full of admiration for them, at least we had a steel tank around us against the enemy fire but there was no bullshit, no smart drill they just got about the job in hand in a workmanlike fashion"

The armour in the woods consisted of Mk V Panther tanks and the fire from "B" Squadron damaged 2, but at the cost of 6 of their own and with the loss of two crewmen. As for the East Lanc's;

> "I don't remember any of the troops in front falling, but as I was concentrating on looking forward to see targets that's not surprising."

The position was duly taken and the advance continued into the next day until halted by a blown bridge, but the obstacle was quickly breached and the fight went on;

> "We were closely missed by more AP's in five or six seconds than I care to remember .....[but] later in the day we were able to send a few return packets."

The armour piercing shells drove 4 Baker off the road and there followed a rather frantic time of manoeuvring and returning fire, during which a whole row of telegraph poles were demolished causing a couple of infantrymen to hastily vacate the safety of their slit trench. This resulted in the unattached contents of the tank whizzing around inside and as a consequence they briefly became 'hors de combat';

> "We had been moving forwards along a straight road, which rose towards the horizon where there was a thin wood, not many trees but a lot of shrubs, behind a couple of fields.
>
> All at once we came under 88mm fire and pulled off the road, eventually ending up between a barn and farmhouse which were set at right-angles to the '88' position. There was about enough space for 2 or 3 tanks and so we moved to the other side of the buildings to see if we could get a line on the '88' from a different angle. It was then we realised that the gun was jammed and had to run it against a wall to operate the recoil and release the steel helmet that had become lodged in the breech."

As they approached the other end though;

> "A machine-gunner somewhere in the fields opposite opened up on us and then the mortars started. As we were 'stuck', at least for a while, Jack jumped out to check there were no Gerries in the buildings. Well there were no Gerries, but the buildings turned out to be an abandoned Gerry Quartermaster's Store. There was ham, bacon, horsemeat, eggs, butter - allsorts.
>
> Anyway, as he came back to tell us there was another hail of machine gun fire so I told him to stay where he was and then Frank jumped out and ran across too. Between them they brewed up and prepared a feast such as we hadn't seen in ages, food hadn't been short but we were so far advanced that Gerry had cut our lines of communication and proper supplies hadn't been getting up.
>
> When it was all prepared the rest of us bailed-out and made a dash through the bullets. Just for a brew and a feed! I had left the headset hanging over the side of the tank with the volume turned up to maximum so we could hear if there were any messages and we just gorged ourselves.
>
> That was the first and only time I tasted horsemeat. It was sweet and tasted horrible."

Being on the receiving end of shell and mortar fire was by no means an unusual occurrence and one that had happened often in the past and would occur again. For the most part the men would take whatever cover was available or simply continue to carry out their duties as best they could, whilst the shells fell around them.

Now, in the main, the men of the Sherwood Rangers were of the 'practical' variety of soldier, as opposed to the 'professional - by the book' types often seen in film dramatisations and found, more frequently, in the senior regiments of the British army. That's not to say they were poor soldiers, far from it, but these battle hardened troops didn't feel the need for foolish bravado. Everyone was experiencing the same risks, everyone had to take the same chances and, as practical men, there was no further need to 'prove' anything to their colleagues. Concessions were also made with regard to peculiarities in dress, as with John's American tanksuit which "nobody ever bothered about", and with some of the procedural disciplines of the 'professional' army;

> "I heard at the time that Brigadier Prior-Palmer once said, in a half disapproving tone, that if there's a roar, followed by a cloud of dust. And when the dust clears you watch the tanks pass by. If you then hear the clatter of cooking pots and pans hanging off the back of the tanks - they are the Sherwood Rangers. We were practical men, civilian soldiers and maybe we didn't quite have the spit and polish of some, but we did the job just as well."

Reading through memoirs of American troops who were supported by the SRY, they clearly did as the comments are often glowing and frequently attest both to their steadiness under fire and attention to the job in hand. As with everything though, there were exceptions and in this same action;

> "Whilst at the farm near Issum we came under a fairly heavy mortar 'stonk' and as we were all taking cover an Officer in an American tank suit, like mine, appeared in the field in front of us apparently unconcerned at the shells falling around him. The Gerries kept laying down fire until he was finally hit and killed."

The Officer was wearing a tanksuit but John didn't recognise him. When you consider that tanks usually operated at some distance from each other, with Troops and Squadrons keeping very much to themselves whilst in action, this is not very surprising. Indeed;

> "I don't even remember seeing my Squadron Leader's tank in action. I only saw it after the battles. In fact most of the time I only ever saw my

own Troop. We were rarely closer than 15 - 20 yards between tanks in action but with the undulations of the countryside even the closest tanks could disappear from sight."

Doubtless this Officer belonged to another Squadron operating in the same area, but looking back and remembering quite how rough it was then, John now wonders if what he then took as 'swank' was really a case battle fatigue. We will never know.

After a short break for maintenance on the 7th there then followed a spell of indirect fire support for the assault on Alpen. Following which it was a move to Goch for re- fitting in preparation for operation Plunder, the crossing of the Rhine.

NOTES:
1 Initially, many Shermans were powered by a 9 cylinder radial Continental R975 aero engine. However, demand for their use in aircraft forced alternative engines to be found and many of the British M4 Shermans had two General Motors 6046 diesel truck engines positioned either side of the engine compartment - linked to a single transmission axle. Various petrol engined versions still appeared though, either as originally supplied or when engines were salvaged from 'brewed-up' tanks. M4A4 Shermans, which comprised the bulk of the British 'Firefly' force, had a Chrysler WC Multibank petrol engine, made up of five car engines.
2 Slang for the Royal Artillery

CHAPTER 9 - THE FINAL PUSH

For the armour there were to be three ways to cross the Rhine. Squadrons from the Staffordshire Yeomanry were to 'swim' their tanks across using duplex-drive vehicles, just as the SRY had done in the Normandy invasion. The Sherwood Rangers, on the other hand, had two alternative methods allocated - rafting the tanks over or using a class 40 bailey bridge, which was to be built by Sappers, under fire, two days before the tanks were to use it. Whichever option the individual crews drew, there was little doubt it would be a risky job.

During the preparation, therefore, the Regiment tried to instil some confidence in their men and as part of this process most of the crews attended a rafting demonstration. Unfortunately this did little to build confidence as it was fraught with difficulties despite the weather and conditions being near perfect. Indeed, some of the demonstration rafts came close to sinking.

Understandably, therefore, when the great day came it was approached with some trepidation.

D-Day for Operation Plunder had been set for the 24th March and two days later, on schedule, the SRY moved to the marshalling area. Order of march was "B" Squadron in the lead, followed by "RHQ", "C" and then "A" Squadron coming up the rear. Consequently, "B" Squadron tanks had the honour of crossing first and at 0700 hours in the dim light of dawn John moved away from the bank on a raft, called 'tank ferry Tilbury';

> "There were two rafts, each barely large enough for the tank to fit on with only inches to spare on each side, at the back and front. They were side by side on the river and each was pulled across by a hawser, powered by a barrage balloon motor or something similar. Each raft had a motor on each bank, with a hawser attached to each end.
>
> The process was to be that one tank was towed across and whilst it unloaded, the other raft loaded up. Then the first raft was towed back empty as the second was towed over full. That way there was only one tank on the water at any one time in case of heavy shell fire. A little further down there was another set of rafts and the distance across was about half a mile.

When we came to loading our tank it had to be lined up perfectly and was then driven straight from the bank onto the raft. If it was not in line, the first track to touch would lift one side of the raft and you had to start again. For the procedure I stood at the far end of the raft and guided the tank on by holding up both arms, fists clenched, and signalling 'left stick', 'right stick' by raising and lowering my arms. I was stood right on the very edge and the tank had to actually touch me before it was fully in place. To move round the side you had to walk sideways, it was that tight a fit.

As we moved away, all the crew climbed out and sat on top because they reckoned that if we were hit then we wouldn't stand a chance if it went in. That said, when we were about a third of the way across a couple of salvos were fired at the crossing site, the nearest landing about 50 yards away. I watched them land, then turned to the others to comment - only to find that they had all jumped back inside!"

Apart from those few rounds, the crossing was uneventful and on the whole the experience had been quite an anti- climax when they finally reached the other side. Once disembarked though, the action became intense and continued well into the night;

"..... the air was thick with steel, but Blue Light Special had a charmed life and came through in her usual way. Clearing some woods a little later we fired belt after belt of Browning at spots where we thought Gerry would be. After a lull some twenty or thirty Gerries made a dash in the open for cover. Jack [Snedker] swung [the] gun and stamped on the button - but no, she just wouldn't work. Frank [Milner] was excited and the I-C crackled, "For christ's sake shoot 'em, you're letting them go" The Browning was working again in a matter of seconds but those chaps certainly owed their lives to that stoppage."

They certainly did, for a short while later Sergeant Sage and his crew took them prisoner.

For the crossing and subsequent attack on the town of Rees, "B" Squadron's losses were limited to just one tank suffering mechanical failure - their good fortune was holding. The next day 4 Troop was detached in support of some infantry plagued by self-propelled guns and John found himself in one of those 'coincidences of war'.

The unit they supported was the 2nd Battalion, the Seaforth Highlanders.

The same unit his elder brother Tom served with in the Great War.

Pressing on, the action moved to Isselburg and on the 28th;

> "..... during [a] terrific rain of shells, we had two or three drop within six
> feet ..... and one exploded on the back with serious effect to the rations.
> Jack [Snedker] made a hurried dive underneath, and we all had to bale out,
> the cordite fumes were choking."

They had been hit by a mortar shell but fortunately the damage had been limited to the bedding and rations stacked neatly behind the turret. It had landed only a couple of feet behind the open butterfly lids, the second time a shell had fallen that close - the long odds they played seemed to be paying off, as other than a brief spell of coughing there had been no casualties. And all of this despite it being recorded by Captain Leinster that;

> '..... Cpl Cropper [was] always well up ....'

Later that day the action moved back over the border into Holland to the town of Dinxperlo, which fell after about 15 hours of close action during the afternoon of the 29th. It was now time for a short rest;

> "The Dutch people were always very friendly and helpful, despite the
> damage we caused during the fighting. Rest stops in Holland were always
> popular."

All the more so because the civilians readily helped to supplement rations without prompting. They would share things with the troops without looking for payment, though they normally received it - unlike many of the French that John encountered;

> "You traded with the French. For instance we would swop one of those
> small 2oz bars of dark chocolate for a litre of milk at a farm and then heat
> it up with another 2oz bar shaved into it. It made a sort of cocoa drink
> which made a change from compo tea. With compo, sometimes it was OK
> and other times it wasn't so good at all."

Whilst at rest orders were received giving the next objective - Bremen. The route was to mean crossing the border between Holland and Germany on more than one occasion, and another crossing of the Rhine. It was no surprise, therefore, that when they eventually moved out on the 1st April to take a bridge over the Twente canal they met opposition time and time again as rearguard units constantly impeded their advance.

Days were long and as usual sleep was at a premium. Before the next rest though there was one more task to perform, the liberation of a Dutch town called Hengelo.

After the liberation in Hengelo. The two soldiers are Jack Snedker, left, and John on the right. The woman seated next to John is Marie Kroeze and her 'part' husband Koos is the man looking over Jack's shoulder.

The attack commenced on the 2nd April, but as the tanks finally closed on the outskirts of the town on the 3rd resistance began to crumble. As they entered the streets though opposition became fierce again, but this time it was not the retreating Germans who held up the advance but throngs of civilians, jubilant at their liberation. Casualties for the occupation had been limited to just one Officer, who had been wounded in the hand. He was recovered by some happy Dutch civilians who carried him away to tend his wound in a warm living room somewhere. Likewise a Trooper, whose wound was nothing more serious than a wet battledress blouse. It seemed as though the whole population wanted to embrace the liberators and with this euphoric welcome it was not to be until 1 a.m. on the 4th before the Germans were finally cleared out.

Once the town was safe the response of the 3000 citizens of Hengelo to their liberation by the British was overwhelming, with every house wanting a 'Towmee' billeted on them. An opportunity the men of the SRY happily took as they were to have a few days rest before moving on;

> "It certainly made a change from some of the rest breaks we'd taken over the past few months. I remember once when we pulled back for a rest whilst with the XXIVth, right next to a battery of 5.5's. It was the 12th July '44 and the first time we had slept outside the tanks for weeks. We stretched a tarpaulin from the side of the tank to the floor and settled in our bedding, fully clothed of course, for a proper nights rest.

> But the damn battery put up a barrage all night. There was a constant whistling and whining over our heads - we never got any rest at all.

> On another occasion after a pretty hard spell, we finally reached the rest area for a three day break when we were ordered to go back because they needed us!"

When they eventually moved away on the 9th it was in many ways a sad parting. But plenty of new friends had been made and contact between the liberators and the citizens of Hengelo was to continue for a long time to come;

> "I slept in the tank for the first night there, as did the rest of the crew because Gerry was not that far away and there was a threat of a counter attack. That said, we were 'adopted' by the Kroeze family. We used to go

there to eat, taking our rations and tea, which they hadn't seen for years. They used to add fresh vegetables and potatoes and do the cooking, and we always left plenty of food behind. All through the campaign, food was the one thing we were never short of.

The daughter of the house, Marie, and her husband were only 'part' married by the Dutch system. Apparently they hold both a civil and a church ceremony and they had only undergone the civil one. I got a letter from her much later that year saying that they had finally 'got married' on the 9th August. That same letter brought some sad news as well."

Marie had a brother, also called John, who was killed by an allied vehicle in a crash whilst riding his motorbike shortly after the liberation. This young man had been one of the many Dutch people who had continued to resist the occupation of their country, particularly with regard to 'downed' allied air crew whom he hid from the German army on numerous occasions. Corporal Cropper first learned of this resistance from another source though;

"I had been sat chatting to this chap in civvies whilst in Hengelo when I suddenly realised that he spoke English without the pronounced foreign accent of the locals. "You speak damn good English!" I said, as much in praise as anything else, "I ought to" he replied, "I am English." It turned out that he was an RAF Sergeant who had been shot down and had been hidden in the town by John Kroeze and his companions."

It transpired that Marie and her brother had another sideline as well - she would lure unsuspecting Germans into dark alleys, he made sure they stayed there - permanently!

As they moved on from such happy surroundings, progress was again hampered by enemy rearguards and with "B" Squadron once more at the head of the march they took their share of casualties. Another three tanks were 'brewed-up' over the next two days. By the 11th they were still leading, this time at the very front of the whole British advance together with infantry support from 130 Brigade. They passed through Herzlake but as usual quickly encountered troops armed with the ubiquitous Panzerfausts in the surrounding area. In an attempt to press on they bypassed the occupied zone and moved on to Lonningen - where yet more Panzerfausts appeared. Resistance was fierce as the Squadron pressed on into the nearby woods to clear out the opposition and make a firebase.

Two more tanks had already been lost and it seemed inevitable that more would fall victim. The odds at survival appeared to be shortening.

> "Outside Cloppenburg [on the 13th April] we fired at 3500 yards range and registered hits on infantry concentrations. In fact we almost ran out of H.E. Gerry replied with A.P., but he didn't find us, his nearest shot was some five yards away."

The tanks then pressed on into the town itself with "B" Squadron taking up the lead, and "4" troop forming the spearhead. At the very front was 4 Baker;

> "In the town we [passed] S.P.s with muzzle covers on [and] destroyed an A.P. gun [shaking] the nerves of the crews [around us]."

It was then that fate took a hand. Cloppenburg lay on either side of a river and 4 Troop's leader, Lt Hyde, found one bridge that had not been demolished. He ordered his troop across to break the ground for the infantry and 4 Baker led the way again. After an initial firefight;

> "We finally ran out of H.E. so had to pull over to let the tank behind take the lead. It was [Sgt] 'Shoey' Sage's, and he hadn't gone more than a few yards past when he came to a road block and was hit by a Panzerfaust and killed."

To date the crew of Blue Light Special had been lucky, but the luck didn't last very much longer;

> "Jack and Frank went out to try and bring in the crew. Only Frank came back, and we returned to a farmhouse for the night very much saddened. We were all so much one it hadn't seemed as if anything could separate us."

The Adjutant, Captain Leinster, who also served in "B" Squadron recorded much of the events of that time and finally summarised this last action by simply saying that Lt Hyde's Troop had a very dirty hour in the eastern end of town. It was not just the crew of 4 Baker who were subdued that night.

Down to a crew of three, Bill Jackson joined them to act as gunner and 4 Baker stayed in action for the next few days whilst the Regiment closed on Bremen. However;

"..... [we] missed the entry into Bremen, the only action [the tank] missed whilst in our hands. Ted had gone on leave and Bill was sick but he elected to remain with us."

As they prepared to rejoin the fray, the end was now drawing near.

"My instructions were to move off at leisure and join up with the Tank Collection Point. Our idea of leisure proved eventually to be mid-day, and of course the T.C.P. had gone. After a delay of a couple of hours or more the Light Aid Detachment provided us with the location and two more tanks to take up. We set out [at some speed and eventually] in the distance we saw five tanks hull down. Investigation proved that they were [the] T.C.P., almost turret down in the mud. Here we got a more up to date location but decided to harbour for the night. The following morning ..... we set out in the rain and caught up ..... ."

A typical view of a troop laager, surrounded by the flotsam of military life. Note the bicycle propped against one of the tanks, known to the men as Frank's farrad (the German for bicycle). Liberated by Frank Milner in the course of the advance,

The area they were passing through was not fully secure so the company of two other tanks was welcomed. But;

> "They were clearly in no hurry to reach the front and kept falling behind, which would have left us without support if anything had happened. I suppose with being battle hardened we didn't see the risks in the same way, or at least we assessed them differently."

Fortunately the trip was without any excitement and upon arrival at the Regiment;

> "..... we were joined by 'Mac' and set out to join the Squadron, which we did in the evening. ..... [he] was just out of England and was a little shy but he was very keen. He became Gunner and Bill, Operator.
>
> Once more we were doing flying column work and our troop left its usual trail of fires and destruction. Those were the days of mines and bazookas [and we] picked our way in and out of them ..... even one night when somebody cut the floor from under us ..... [we] just ploughed on."

It was clear that resistance was faltering and it became common to see disarmed German soldiers walking slowly back through the allied lines, trying to find a collection point for prisoners. More unusually;

> "As we pressed forward there came a point when we were capturing more than we were killing but couldn't afford the manpower to take care of the prisoners. The solution, therefore, was to load them on the back of the tanks as we continued to press forward.
>
> Certainly the ones I had on my tank from time to time were not happy with this as we were under constant fire from their compatriots. To be honest, I was a little uneasy as well because they had only been casually searched and if one of them had a knife it would have been easy to stick it in my back. For my part though, despite my fears, I was always occupied with the business of war and paid them little attention."

It was now the 4th May and the Squadron went out to support the 7th Hants and 4th Wiltshire's in the crossing of a canal at Hamme. The rumour was that the Burgemeister of a village on the other side of the canal had ordered all arms to be handed in at the Rathaus (Town Hall) and it was hoped to take the ground with no loss. Unfortunately the tanks could find no way of crossing the canal so the infantry pressed on alone.

This sudden change in plan was recorded at the time in terms of the crews being frustrated at being unable to cross. Doubtless, in a sense, they were but the reality of not having to go yet again into an area of risk was recorded differently by John:

> "..... [frankly] we couldn't care less about not being able to cross, in fact we were pleased that we were not going into action and felt relieved when we pulled away."

That night the armour consolidated in the Narrenburg area, with "B" Squadron laagering in an old fruit orchard some distance from the rest of the Regiment;

> "We pulled into the remnants of [the] orchard to laager for the night and there were rumours flying around that the Germans had packed in - that they had surrendered or wanted to surrender. The following morning ..... it was here that the war for us came to an end, all German forces opposing 21st Army Group surrendered."

At 20.30 hours on May 4th 1945, the order was received that all resistance had ceased in the British Zone. Three days later at 41 minutes past 2 on the morning of 7 May, the final surrender was signed.

*Taken the morning after Cloppenburg. Back row - Birch, Bob Evans,
Frank Milner, McAvish, Ted King, Neil, Peate and Rob. Front row, John,
Jock, Lt. Richard Hyde, Gordon and Davies. In the background is the Blue
Light Special and the photograph was taken by the only other 4 Troop
survivor, Sgt. Robbo Roberts.*

*Although many are smiling, John remembers this as one of the most
unhappy days they experienced with the people just milling around with
little or nothing to say. Lost in silent depression.*

CHAPTER 10 - FAREWELL OLD FRIEND

For the men of "RHQ" Squadron who got confirmation on the night of the 4th, the relief was absolute. The night sky was lit by a combination of Very lights and 'artificial moonlight'[1] flashing across the sky, with more than one bottle of intoxicating liquor suddenly appearing. "B" Squadron didn't receive their confirmation until early on the morning of the 5th though and their reaction was a little different;

> "It was instant relief - no wild cheering or running about. It was a case of 'thank God it's all over' and we were safe at last. We had nothing to celebrate with anyway, just compo tea and normal rations. It was as if you'd had an exhausting day and you flop down in a chair at the end of it with the relief that it was all over."

In fact the only gesture of celebration John made involved;

> "..... throwing away a cheap metal ring I had found a few months earlier. I had worn it as a sort of lucky charm during the past months and somehow I didn't feel I needed it anymore."

In addition;

> "I had been told a few weeks earlier that my tank was to be fitted with rockets and had even been given instructions on how to use them. I now realised that this wasn't to be."

The actual surrender was effective from 0800 hours that morning and there then followed a week's wait in this location until 'policing' duties could be sorted out. During that time;

> "We stripped the camouflage from BLS and could hardly recognise her. On her side were huge white letters ..... proclaiming her name to all and sundry."

There then followed a small Victory parade at Wesermunde, which was as much a show of force as anything else, and then a spell of guard duties dealing, in the main, with large numbers of looters and acts of drunken behaviour. Particularly with displaced Poles, Russians and other nationalities

At a pause in the march. Note the bedding stacked at the back of the turret and the branches and logs attached around the tank.

who had formerly been engaged as slave workers in the area. A role John found not unfamiliar.

Curiously, as the Regiment moved into their new area they were met by crowds of German civilians lining the streets and cheering, almost as if they were being liberated. Totally unexpected and in a sense rather unnerving;

> "The billeting worked on the basis of the number of rooms in a house. Occupants were allowed the minimum number of rooms for personal use and the rest were used as billets. We, in turn, were instructed not to talk to the Germans once billeted. Anyway, I was given a billet in a house with an elderly widow in her 60's and she kept away from us, but tidied the house when we weren't around.
>
> One day I walked in and a couple of the lads said the lady of the house wants to have a word. It turned out that she had a couple of visiting nieces who spoke English and wanted to practice it.
>
> Of course I asked them why the cheering when we arrived and the reason was that they had been told that the Russians were coming, so expected them to take over. They were so relieved when it was British troops arriving that the cheering was spontaneous. The retreating German soldiers had apparently told the people to stay where they were because the British weren't 'barbars' (barbarians) and they should arrive first."

On the 31st May General Sir Brian Horrocks[2], addressed the 8th Armoured Brigade in Hanover and told them that they had seen more fighting than any other armoured brigade since the D-Day landings;

> "Which was a surprise to me because I thought it had been the same for everyone."

He also decorated a number of Officers and N.C.O.s, amongst whom was Captain Leinster[3] who almost crossed paths with John and his crew on the day of the surrender when;

> "Two of the lads were moving our tank and whilst guiding it round, with a flick of the left track, [they] neatly deposited [his] carefully prepared lunch in the bottom of a well. Apparently his crew saw what happened and were quite put out because they had to split their rations to make it up. For some reason they didn't drop us in it though - perhaps the euphoria of the day?"

On the 7th June the tanks were loaded on to transporters for a move to Magdeburg;

> "To take custody of our well known opponents the 15th Panzer Grenadiers. [Whilst there] she was given a coat of green paint and emerged with a brand new name 'Berjou'. A name, incidentally by which she was never recognised. In the Victory parade at Bremerhaven she sailed by in a cloud of dust, just one more tank in a parade."

Not all of the crews had originally given names to their tanks or support vehicles. The "RHQ" Squadron named their vehicles after Sherwood Forest characters when tanks were first issued to the Regiment in 1942 and these names were transferred to replacement vehicles as they were issued, but for the rest of the Squadrons, naming tanks was left to personal preference. Over the passage of years, many of these names have been forgotten and those standing the test of time are now pitifully few. The only names I have been able to trace for the European campaign are;[4]

"R.H.Q." Squadron :

The names used by the 'RHQ' Squadron were originally used when the Regiment received its first tanks during the desert campaign in 1943. As the vehicles were changed the names remained constant and, of these, I have only been able to confirm five.

ROBIN HOOD	-	The Regiment's Commanding Officer's tank, ultimately commanded by Lt. Col Christopherson.
MAID MARION	-	Crew and vehicle unconfirmed.
LITTLE JOHN	-	Crew and vehicle unconfirmed.
ALAN A DALE	-	Crew and vehicle unconfirmed.
FRIAR TUCK	-	Crew and vehicle unconfirmed.

"A" Squadron :

AKILLA	-	A 75mm gunned M4A2 Sherman, no. T146929 commanded by Sgt Dring 'MM and bar' (one of the most celebrated members of the regiment) and crewed by Corporal Gold and Troopers Hodkin, Denton and Bennett.
ARROW	-	Crew and vehicle unconfirmed.

B" Squadron :

PIN UP GIRL	-	A 75mm M4A2 which joined the regiment from the XXIVth Lancers on 4 August 1944. Commanded by Corporal Cropper and crewed by Troopers Tutin, Richardson, Gasson and Cornish.

BLUE LIGHT SPECIAL - A 75mm M4A2 no: T 232668 delivered on 14 August 1944 in replacement of the above. Crewed by the same men, it was destroyed at Geilenkirchen on 19 September 1944 whilst under the command of Lt Charles.

This name was also given to her replacement, a 17pdr M4A1 hybrid no: T 269979, also commanded by Corporal Cropper but crewed, at various times, by Troopers Snedker, Milner, Jackson, King, McFarlane, Machardie and, possibly, Baker.

LILY MARLENE - Crew and vehicle unconfirmed.

BERLIN OR BUST - Crew and vehicle unconfirmed. Whilst painted on to a tank of B Squadron, this may have been more of a statement than a tank name.

"C" Squadron :

BARDIN COLLOS - A 75mm gunned M4A2 Sherman DD commanded by Lt Stuart Hills and crewed by Corporal Footitt and Troopers Kirman, Reddish and Storey. This tank was launched from an L.C.T. on D-Day 6th June 1944 under fire about 700 yards from Gold beach. It made barely a few yards before shipping water and sinking due, it was believed, to damage from shell fire. The crew escaped but presumably the tank still sits where she settled on the sea bed.

CALLIGULA - Crew and vehicle unconfirmed.

COMPANULA - Crew and vehicle unconfirmed.

For the Victory parade, all the vehicles received new names taken from the Regiment's battle honours and were treated with yet another coat of green paint, followed by a set of "squares and symbols"[5] on their sides. They cut a dashing sight when carrying out their duties, a far cry from the mud and camouflaged shapes the crews had become familiar with over the past 12 months.

> "The patrols in Hanover and Ricklingen were carried out with still the same old zest, and B.L.S. put her head down and kicked up her heels in get-a-ways that were just as snappy as when 88's whistled past her tail. She used to come in laden with prisoners and her menacing roar warned all and sundry to get off the streets at curfew time. Pilfering Italians were transfixed when [she bore] down on them, and after a crude justice was administered she would carry them in [to] the office of 'Herr Commandant'.

> After Hanover, apart from long journeys, some by road, some on transporters ..... we saw less of her. We painted , polished and washed her down, but we weren't doing things together. At Einbeck she gave signs of her strenuous past by throwing off connectors"

During this time the crew of 'Blue Light Special' increased somewhat;

> "Ted had come back from leave, but as we were no longer taking casualties there was no place for him so to keep him from the FDS I swung it so that he could stay with the crew. Around the same time I also took [R] McFarlane on as well, he was an old 4 Troop boy from the XXIVth."

Total crew, therefore, 6 - in a tank designed for 4. Needless to say, 2 usually rode on the back.

It was not all work though. On the 15 July John got a spot of Paris leave to break the monotonous policing duties. A little later he also got away for a trip of a different kind, to get a closer look at what the war was all about;

> "A chance came to visit one of the Concentration camps so I thought I should go and have a look. It was to be quite a journey but I felt I should make the effort - quite a few of us went in the end.

> By the time we arrived the place had been fairly well cleaned up but there was still a risk of disease, so before we were allowed in they took some bellows and squirted powder into every nook and cranny. Up sleeves,

trouser legs, down trousers, necks and pockets. There was white powdery dust everywhere.

As for the camp itself, all the bodies had been buried and lots of the ovens had been cleaned out. On the whole, the people left in the camp were not looking too bad. There were people milling around and still tidying up, but a lot of the place was derelict.

They had a big picture display with whole plate sized photographs, showing the Germans digging graves and burying what would have been nothing more than living 'skeletons' when they were alive. I'm glad I went to see it."

One of the clearest photographs taken on the visit to the concentration camp. This tranquil setting belies the horrors that went on here.

Paris, on the other hand, was as full of life as it had always been;

"It was only a two day pass but I crammed in as much as I could. I stayed in Ronceray Church, Army Hostel - bed number 3 in room 66. There were lots of beds and people of all units everywhere.

Whilst there I managed a coach tour of the city, to see the sights, and also saw the shows at the Folies Bergere and Casino de Paris. I even did a bit of window shopping and had a look around the Louvre."

It was now September and the last three months had been spent alternating between rounding up Nazis, maintaining civil peace and playing inter-unit football matches. But on the 18th a momentary lapse of concentration led to the following item appearing in the regimental broad sheet, the Sherwood Siren;

> From our "B" Squadron reporter.
>
> The friends of Cpl. Cropper will regret to hear that he has been admitted to hospital as the result of a suspected fractured ankle. Johnny certainly found out that a half-track vehicle weighs too much when it runs over your foot.

Fortunately only a small bone was broken and John was soon to be back with the Troop, albeit with a plaster cast, but at the age of 76 years he still suffers from a fallen arch caused by that chance encounter.

On the 2nd October a final diary entry is made, perhaps indicative of a member of a unit unused to the spit and polish of the more senior regiments such as those in the Guards divisions;

> " ..... [the tank] is now being prepared for her part in the last parade. Gallons of diesel oil flow from her hull and a white paint brush touches odd bolt heads. She doesn't like it, nor do we, we were happier together when she carried us on our duties. Soon she will leave us going to whom or what we do not know. With us she will take some of our spirit, but I doubt if it will ever be remembered as it was with us. Instead of Blue Light Special she will be T269979. It sounds cold and cruel, but wherever she goes she will be remembered by the six men who will watch her rear disappearing into the distance. ..... Good-bye old girl, we won't forget you."

The Blue Light Special. Cleaned and ready for parade.

On the actual day of the final parade, 3rd October 1945, a letter from a tank crew appeared in the Sherwood Siren;

To the Editor   "B" Sqn S.R.Y.

In writing these few lines, we are trying to express the sentiments of the majority of us on the loss of our tanks. Most of us who are "tank men" have slept, fought, and eaten in these vehicles for a greater proportion of the past 12 months, and, as a result, have developed a strong affection for them. In fact they have literally been our homes. They carried our beds, our food and such comforts as we were able to acquire on the journey through the war. It is small wonder then, that we have a genuine affection for them. We all know that, generally, we condemn them and find numerous faults with them, but every member of a crew always ends his condemnation with some redeeming feature. It is because of this redeeming feature that we love them, - how much, we only found out on being told that we were to lose them.

In addition to the tanks, which might be regarded as a foundation of our present lives, we have built up a splendid spirit of friendship, comradeship and loyalty. This spirit has indeed become so mighty in strength that we would venture to suggest that nothing can destroy it, not even the removal of that foundation - the tank. They will take the tank, we can't stop that, but the spirit will go on forward again making the best of whatever befalls. We will remember the tanks and say, "we did it before, we can do it again." It is nevertheless with deep regret that we say "good-bye" to a comrade of 1000 miles of action. She never let us down.

The old "Blue Light Special"
Sincerely yours,
The Crew.

Its author, John Cropper.

The tanks were then loaded on to transporters for the last time as the crews bade their final farewell. By 8th October the first releases began and by early December John was on his way home to England.

"Our tank was so worn out that on our way to hand her in she lost two or three spuds [track links], with them flying 30 or 40 yards through the air. We did 1000 miles of action in that tank with no major problems and she still managed that last trip without having to do any track bashing."

As for the Sherwood Rangers Yeomanry, in April 1946 they were put into suspended animation just as with the legendary King Arthur, to await the time when England again would be in need.[6]

Loading 'Berjou' for her final journey.

NOTES:
1 Provided by the 1127th Searchlight Battery
2 Commander 30 Corps from 3rd August 1944
3 Receiving the Croix de Guerre
4 The XXIVth Lancers also named their vehicles and other than 'Pin up Girl' I have managed to trace the following; 'A' Squadron - Arran, 'B' Squadron - Bloody Mary, Black Prince, Butcher Cumberland, Buq Buq and The Ram, 'C' Squadron - Charlie.
5 For Blue Light Special, the symbols consisted of a white, hollow square on the turret, a tactical mark on the hull (53 on a red square) and the brigade sign - a Fox's mask. The square identified the tank as belonging to 'B' Squadron with the colour, white, signifying the third regiment in the brigade.
6 Official notification of disbandment was received on 1 February 1946 and by 28th February the Regiment had been fully dispersed, but not before receiving the Freedom of the city of Nottingham. As fate would have it, the Sherwood Rangers Yeomanry were re-formed in the 1960's in their old 'Yeomanry' role as a T.A. unit and ultimately they became 'B' (Sherwood Rangers Yeomanry) Squadron, The Queens Own Yeomanry. In 1994, the 200th year of the Yeomanry, they were to exercise their right to march through the City of Nottingham - watched, perhaps for the last time, by 29 men who had fought with them in the Second World War. John stood amongst them.

CHAPTER 11 - AND BACK TO BLUE

At a time when literally thousands of servicemen were being demobilised, the process was, perhaps understandably, without much ceremony or feeling. It was just a case of volume processing and it left a bitter taste in John's mouth.

Upon arrival back in England he was first sent to Catterick for four days, then he had a couple of days home leave following which it was back to the camp for final de-mobilisation. However;

> "They treated us like rubbish and even applied barrack charges for breakage's when we hadn't broken anything. It was diabolical. There was no appreciation for all we'd been through. We'd risked death, seen friends and colleagues die - we didn't look for praise or adulation but there was no justification for how were handled."

This was not an isolated incident either. A number of ex-SRY men had similar experiences.

Released finally on the afternoon of the 20th he caught a train to Liverpool and eventually stepped on to Victoria station shortly after midnight, a civilian at last. There then followed a 12 mile walk home, but it was a clear night and somehow the 3 hours it took seemed to fly by.

What thoughts went through his mind during that walk have long since been lost in memory, but doubtless they reflected the past 2 years and unquestionably they turned to his colleagues in that great adventure:

In 'Pin Up Girl' there was the Corporal who despite his nerve having been broken in the actions fought during the days after the invasion, still had the strength to realise that he was a threat to both the crew and himself and so reported sick.

Then there was 'Ritchie' Richardson, the driver who turned up at Louvain Hospital badly burnt with the sad news of the rest of the crew. 'Toots' Tutin, who survived the 'brew-up', and Fred 'Gassy' Gasson, who didn't. And finally Keith Cornish, who was as un- military as anyone could be, insisted on calling everybody 'old boy' and who turned down the opportunity of escaping the front line and going to Officer Training Corps to stay with his pals and die on the Siegfried line.

These last 4 also made the first 'Blue Light Special' their home as well.

'Blue Light Special', the second, became a home to Jack Snedker who died trying to save his colleagues at Cloppenburg and Frank Milner who's D.I.Y. turned an otherwise lumbering tank into an extremely nippy one. Bill Jackson, the one who chose to stay with the tank instead of taking sick leave, 'Mac', the quiet boy from England, Ted King who sat on the back of 'Pin Up Girl' cooking a chicken and, finally, the old XXIVth Trooper who came across to the SRY with John back in August 1944, 'Mac' McFarlane.

There had also been Lt. Hyde, the sort of chap you'd follow anywhere, and 'Shoey' Sage, who traded places and suffered the ultimate consequences. Poor old 'deaf' Sergeant Carr and Harry Thomas, who was never on net. Sergeant 'Robbo' Roberts, commander of 4 Able, Pete Taylor, who survived hostilities only to step on a mine guiding a tank through a gate some weeks later, and 'Paddy' Costello, Sergeant's Birch and Collis, Corporal's Turner and Fyfe, Lance Corporal's Lear and Bainbridge, Troopers Heavans, Rose, Brown, Nimmo, Randle, Stapley and Treadgold ..... the list goes on. Some didn't make it. Others, like John, were also on their way home - the dead remembered, the living forgotten. But not by those with whom they served.

'Mac' Machardie

Bill Jackson

As John closed the door behind him in the early hours of the 21st December the next stage of his life was about to begin and his memories, writings and souvenirs were to be locked away for almost 48 years until, like Pandora's Box, some inquisitive fingers lifted the lid.

Shortly after Christmas he dusted off his civilian suit and DC1189 returned to duty as a Fingerprint Officer at Seaforth Police Station. In the same way he had done so often before.

The world moved on.

Many, many years later, just following the re-unification of Germany, John took a short holiday in Berlin. His first trip to that country since 1945. At Tegel Airport he was met by the tour guide, who's job it was to see him to his hotel and supply a wealth of leaflets explaining the various sites worth visiting during his stay.

The transfer to the hotel was on a normal service bus and as the two men sat side by side Heinz Pauers, the tour rep, explained some of the sites they could see from the bus as the two men chatted freely. Whilst crossing Kaiser Damm, Heinz began to explain the origin of the attractive and extremely decorative street lighting, put up in honour of a visit by Mussolini over 50 years earlier. Not surprisingly the conversation then turned to the Second World War.

It transpired that Heinz too was a tankman. During the war years he drove Mk III's and Mk IV's, but at the time of the invasion he was serving in a Mk V Panther - thrown time and again against the advancing British and American forces in northern France, Belgium and Holland.

Frank Milner

Some of the many men of "B" Squadron.

There, sat on a bus one winter's evening, amongst people on their way home from a hard day at the office, setting off for a night on the town or simply returning from a days sightseeing, were two men chatting as though they had known each other all their lives. They shared the odd joke, they shared the odd memory and when the bus pulled up outside the hotel they went their separate ways.

Two ordinary men, who once wore different uniforms, stood on different 'sides' of a great divide and shared similar experiences, but neither viewed the other with hatred or malice. Take the politicians away and we are all just people. And we get along just as people always have - and always should.

ADDENDUM

As a military historian, it is the details that are the most important. Those insignificant little things that can explain so much when placed into context. I have tried to fit as many of these in to this record as possible, but inevitably there have been some that for one reason or another ended up being excluded. Of these, I simply could not finish without mentioning the following:

As I have already stressed, life for a tankman in action was a risky business with few managing to go through the whole of the European campaign without some form of injury - just look at the list of the XXIVth Lancers who transferred to the Sherwood Rangers. Of the 28 Officers and men, 9 were killed, 6 wounded and 2 became P.O.W.'s, probably having been wounded in the process - and those are only the ones I managed to get confirmed. The odds were appreciated by the men and sometimes they did seemingly strange things in an effort to lengthen them;

> "When going into action I always wore my earphones with only one of them over an ear, leaving the other ear free to make it easier to hear if anything happened around me. In the noise of battle I don't suppose it would have made a great deal of difference but I was certainly a lot more at ease. Another thing I always did was never to climb down from the turret. I always stood up on top of the turret ring and then jumped down.
>
> It seemed a hell of a way down when you were stood up there, but I thought that if we were ever brewed- up and I had to bail out then there would be less chance of hesitating before jumping off. A moments hesitation could mean the end."

Believe me, it is a long way down. To check out the written specifications for Sherman tanks I visited a company who sells them to collectors and after crawling over one for about half an hour, I stood up on top of the turret and looked down.

I didn't jump.

BIBLIOGRAPHY

Other than the writings and reminisces of John Cropper, direct quotes from which are shown in quotation marks throughout the text, other reference sources are:

o   Assault Crossing - The River Seine 1944: Ken Ford; David and Charles 1988.

o   Assault on Germany - The Battle for Geilenkirchen: Ken Ford; David and Charles 1989.

o   B Squadron Royal Yeomanry (TA) [The Sherwood Rangers Yeomanry] Museum, Cavendish Drive, Carlton, Nottingham.

o   Lancer Life - newsletter of the XXIVth Lancers, 18 July 1944 to 26 July 1944.

o   Merseyside at War - Rodney Whitworth; Scouse Press, 1988

o   Military Collectables - Richard O'Neil; Salamander Books 1983

o   None Had Lances (the story of the 24th Lancers) - Leonard Willis; 24th Lancers Old Comrades Association 1986.

o   Nottinghamshire Sherwood Rangers Yeomanry Welfare Association Reports - April 1945 and December 1945.

o   Sherwood Rangers - T M Lindsay; Burrup, Matthieson & Co., Ltd, London 1952

o   Sherwood Siren - newsletter of the Sherwood Rangers Yeomanry, 3 October 1945 to 24 October 1945.

o   Tank Fist - Dr Stephen Bull, 'Military Illustrated' March 1994.

o   The 8th Armoured Brigade, 1939 - 1945; produced by the 8th Armoured Brigade in Hanover, 1945.

o   The M4 Sherman Tank and its close variants - A study by Yves Buffetaut Published in 'Militaria' Magazine; February & May 1994.

o   War Diaries of the XXIVth Lancers and The Sherwood Rangers Yeomanry - Public Records Office, Ruskin Avenue, Kew, London.

o   World War II: The Sharp End - John Ellis; Windrow & Greene (revised) 1990.

ACKNOWLEDGEMENTS

I am indebted to all those people who have searched through their memories and helped with my research. In particular, those members of the Old Comrades Association's for both the XXIVth Lancers and Sherwood Rangers Yeomanry who managed to recall some of the tank names mentioned in Chapter 10. In addition I would also like to thank Les Mellors and Sergeant Barron ('B' Sqn Queens Own Yeomanry), for their time and patience on the visit with my father, Margaret Gillatt of 'A S Budge' for letting me play with one of their Sherman tanks and Ben and Mave Chapman - good and true friends of many years - for their guidance and encouragement.

And finally - Rob Prior, for the hours of patient frustration spent in setting the text.

To the victors the spoils
Sergeant Robbo Roberts is on the extreme left
holding the corner of the flag